KU-223-955

For my grandson Hugo

Thanks to both my grandfathers,
I have grown up with a love of nature
and of gardening.
I can only hope that my own
enthusiasm might rub off on him,
four generations on.

[signature]
June 2012/.

North Lanarkshire

7 777492 16

ALAN TITCHMARSH

My Secret Garden

A personal tour of my own private plot

PHOTOGRAPHS BY JONATHAN BUCKLEY

North Lanarkshire Council Motherwell Library Hamilton Road, Motherwell MOT	
7 777492 16	
Askews & Holts	16-Nov-2012
635.092	£25.00
	394600

Contents

Introduction

'In all, let Nature
never be forgot.'

Alexander Pope

To be honest, mine is not so much a secret garden as a private one, and that's a bit of a novelty really. Having used our last garden for filming and photography for twenty-odd years, I promised my wife and family when we moved, back in 2002, that the next garden would be just for us.

I felt a bit churlish really. Ungrateful I suppose, since using my garden as a workshop-cum-film set has enabled me to earn a decent living. Not that it was created simply for the cameras; it was *our* garden first and foremost – a *real* garden – and television had to fit in. But the family had tolerated for long enough the fact that it was difficult to recline there in peace on a sunny summer's day, or have a quiet cup of tea on a bench without having to move out of the way for a tripod.

The pleasure of sharing the fruits of our labours is something treasured by British gardeners, which goes some way to explaining why almost 4,000 private and domestic gardens are open under the aegis of the National Gardens Scheme each year. They fling wide their gates to raise money for nursing charities, but also so that their owners can share their pleasure. You could

argue that this reveals more than a degree of showing off, too, but when you've created something beautiful from a patch of grey earth or soggy mud there is an urge to share its beauty with others.

Thanks to *Gardeners' World* I had the chance, each week from February to November, to say to an audience of several million 'Just come and look at this!' It was a great privilege, and a great outlet for anyone with a passion for plants. What's more, the several million left not a single footprint.

Why leave our old garden at 'Barleywood' after twenty-one years? Several reasons. One is that we have always loved Georgian houses – Barleywood was an extended chalet-bungalow. The second reason was that a large part of the garden there was on a north-west-facing one-in-four slope and so was slow to warm up. The soil was a mixture of chalk, clay and flint – fiendishly difficult to cultivate. And, not to put too fine a point on it, we were past fifty. The prospect of being *forced* to move as my body succumbed to the rigours of digging clay was not something I wanted to contemplate. More positively, I also felt that I had one more garden in me.

When our current house came on the market it fitted the bill perfectly – a Georgian farmhouse just a stone's throw from where we already lived, big enough for the two of us (plus the girls when they had families and came to stay), and a relatively level to gently undulating garden that was neither too large nor too small with decent soil – the chalk remains, about a foot-and-a-half below the surface, but there are fewer flints and no clay.

The garden at Barleywood totalled two acres, plus around 35 acres of meadow and woodland that we turned into a nature reserve. When we sold the house and garden we retained the meadow and woodland, which we continue to manage for wildlife and our native flora.

The 'new' house was sold with two acres – three-quarters of an acre of garden proper, in which the house sits, plus an acre and a half of … well, you could call it paddock, but it was basically nettles and long grass. A few years later we managed to buy another two acres, which we turned into a wild flower meadow.

Everything within the four acres, save for a handful of mature trees, has been created and planted within the last ten years. (We bought the house on St George's Day 2002 and moved in on 16 December that year, having had to do rather more restoration work on the house than was originally envisaged.)

So why this book? Well, people kept asking what the 'new' garden was like. (I think some folk thought that without the pressure of a TV camera I wouldn't bother quite so much.) And, to be honest, I missed sharing my triumphs (and disasters) in the way that gardeners do. Did I miss showing off? A bit, I suppose, but not letting people

see what we have created is rather like an actor learning a part and then performing without an audience – the experience is meant to be shared; so are gardens.

And so I struck a deal with Mrs T. The deal was that Jonathan Buckley – a brilliant photographer who has, over the years, become a good friend – would record our progress and I would share my garden in the form of a book. That way the garden would still be private (even though Jonathan was assiduous enough to come around 50 times over a seven-year period) and I would have the pleasure of progressing at my own pace instead of that dictated by filming.

This book is the result. It encapsulates my own passion for gardening and my love of line, form, scale, perspective and colour. It will give you an idea of my tastes and predilections, my whims and fancies, as well as being a soapbox for me to expound a modest amount of my personal garden philosophy. The garden of our first marital home measured 15 foot by 35 foot, so I am well aware of my good fortune in being able to 'move up a bit' and have more space. It is something I never take for granted. That said, the general rules of thumb are just the same, regardless of scale.

I am a gardener who designs a bit, rather than a garden designer. I trained in a parks department and the legacy of that is a liking for striped lawns and trimmed edges. I do have a bit of an obsession with neatness, if I'm honest, and that manifests itself in my preference for balance and symmetry, but within the order I enjoy a degree of chaos, too. I think my garden does betray a few delusions of grandeur – I like urns and finials and other classical touches – but I hope the resulting style is elegant rather than pretentious. You can judge that for yourself.

Because nature interests me as much as cultivated plants, and because I feel a deep-seated responsibility to the earth, we garden organically. The last thing to go was an annual application of 'weed and feed' on the lawn – old habits die hard. But when I saw a blackbird pulling up worms to feed its young from the recently treated lawn, whose moss was blackened and whose dandelions were twisted in their death throes, I decided that enough was enough. The annual lawn feed is now the stalwart blood, fish and bonemeal and I have become adept with an old-fashioned daisy grubber. I have not sprayed to control pests and diseases for over twenty years. Bird food costs a fortune.

My garden is certainly an escape, but an escape to reality; for this, rather than the nightly fare of death and destruction delivered by the news bulletins, is what endures – spring returns each year, summer erupts into a billowing shower of flowers, autumn banishes our failures and our successes in equal measure, and winter provides a yearly cauterisation during which we can plot and plan for next year with the gardener's unfailing optimism.

This is work in progress (for gardens are never finished) and a testament to the hard work of the three people who made it – me, along with Bill and Sue who have worked *Chez Titchmarsh* for twenty-odd years; Sue as a gardener and Bill as … well … everything else. Mrs T has a queenly role – to advise, to encourage and to warn – and there are others who pop in from time to time – Gavin the wondrously agile tree surgeon, and Lawrence, Bill's son, who is a dab hand with the mower (we have a lot of grass).

The garden remains private and is not open to the public, but through the pages of this book you are welcome to squeeze under the gate like Peter Rabbit and take a look at what we've created, after working for ten years in fair weather and foul. I would be less than truthful if I did not admit that I am, from time to time, as exasperated as any other gardener. But then there will come a day when the sun shines and the birds sing – often in spring when the foliage is fresh and unsullied by cruel winds – and I will find it hard to control my emotions. At that moment I know I am where I most like being: at home, among the birds and the blossom, gently pottering in my garden.

Alan Titchmarsh
June 2012

Spring

There is a magical moment in spring when the first weak rays of sunshine catch the nodding, pure white flowers of the snowdrops ...

Introduction

The first snowdrops always produce a sigh of relief. Daft really. You'd think that after fifty-odd years of gardening the thrill of their appearance might have worn off. Surely they are as reliable as the tides? It makes no difference. I still mither. Or get a bit gloomy if they are tardy. Their appearance is a signal that there will indeed be another spring, that I have another chance to enjoy my garden, another chance to get it right, hoping that the year ahead will be even better than the last. That, they say, is the difference between farmers and gardeners: farmers always think it will be worse …

The snowdrops emerge from a grassy bank opposite the kitchen window some time in January or February, depending on the severity of the winter weather. They had been planted before we arrived and surprised us with a generous welcome – in a great arc of glaucous tufts – in February 2003, having betrayed no sign of their presence when we moved in during the previous December. They are a winter flower, really, but since they are always considered to be heralds of spring, I like to think of them as the first flower to open in the garden rather than the last.

Aside from 'snowdrop', *Galanthus nivalis* has interesting common names: 'February fair-maids' is the most poetic, but in Yorkshire it is sometimes called 'snow piercer' – a reference to the reinforced sheath above the flower which has the capability of pushing up through the snow's frozen crust. It is the plain single variety that grows in our grassy bank – more graceful than the double form, which reminds me of those ladies on *Strictly Come Dancing* with their layers of sequinned tulle. I have planted more

clumps outside the front gates (always more successful when moved 'in the green' during March rather than as dry and often desiccated bulbs in autumn), and I try a few named varieties such as 'Viridapice' and 'Ophelia' in clay pots for the table outside the kitchen window. But they seem happiest when let loose in the earth where they multiply at a much faster rate, probably because when in their pots I can forget to water them and they are no lovers of drought.

The 'Tommies' emerge slightly later – the amethyst spears of *Crocus tommasinianus* that we planted like clusters of chorus girls in front of the snowdrops. In sunshine they open into brilliant stars, but I love the promise of their intricately veined buds almost more than their open flowers.

To follow there are plenty of dwarf narcissi. I prefer these to the beefier 'cooking daffs' – 'King Alfred' and 'Carlton' – whose robust flowers do a nose-dive when snow or rain weighs heavily upon them, allowing them to be rasped away by slugs and snails that transform their flared trumpets into half-eaten brandy-snaps. This seldom

The amethyst spears of *Crocus tommasinianus* push up through the rough grass in March.

happens to the likes of pale sulphur 'Lemon Silk', ever-reliable 'Tête-à-tête', the elegant 'Apricot', with its pale salmon trumpet, and the angelic milk-white 'Thalia'. They are possessed of far more elegance and their foliage is not nearly so obtrusive in the six weeks that it has to be left intact after the flowers fade, before being scissored off at the ground. In reality, by then the border perennials are rising up to hide the daffs' embarrassment and I hardly notice their withering leaves.

My garden is not so extensive that I can follow Gertrude Jekyll's dictum and have different areas devoted to the respective seasons – a spring garden, a summer border, a winter wonderland. Like most folk I like all my beds and borders to look presentable all the year round, but there are patches – swathes, if you like – in these beds and borders that look especially good in spring.

Farthest from the house, in a curving border near the brick-and-flint wall, are Lenten hellebores. Lots of them. In single and double forms. All different.

I worked oodles of garden compost and well-rotted manure into the ground before planting them, but now it seems hard and unyielding beneath its mulch of chipped bark, which makes a great seedbed for their progeny. The situation doesn't seem to worry them. They still push up and the clumps expand each year, seeming not to mind our flint-ridden chalky earth. Occasionally that black disfiguring fungal disease will attack the odd clump. If the damage is slight I snip off the affected areas; if more widespread then the whole clump is dug up, wrapped in a bin liner and disposed of. Better to be safe …

Beneath the hellebores are sheets of *Cyclamen coum*. I worried at first that the effect was a bit too reminiscent of vibrant summer bedding, but after a long, hard winter, I set aside my shameful snobbery and enjoyed the jolly show. 🌱

Above the hellebores and cyclamen the small but sweetly scented flowers of *Lonicera fragrantissima* (left) speckle the shrub's bare branches. Double and single Lenten hellebores (*Helleborus* x *hybridus*) – many of them contrastingly spotted – open above a bright carpet of *Cyclamen coum* (right).

The drive

A mixture of evergreen shrubs flanked the drive when we bought the house – mahonia, aucuba, *Viburnum tinus* and the like – and although they offered some form of privacy they created an atmosphere that was dark, oppressive and too much like a cemetery for my liking. I thought of planting a great bank of laurel and trimming it into a rolling sea, as they have at Rousham in Oxfordshire where it was planted by that great Georgian designer and architect William Kent. The very name 'laurel' has a funereal Victorian ring to it, but at Rousham it is clipped in an undulating pattern to waist height each year and reflects the light spectacularly. But the space was rather too small and in the end I plumped for box. Had I realised the damage that would be wreaked in the years to come by the deadly box blight I might have plumped for *Choisya ternata* (Mexican orange blossom), which is much beefier but withstands clipping well. It also smothers itself with fragrant white flowers in spring and again, to a lesser extent, in late summer. But then without the benefit of hindsight …

Occasionally patches of my 'waves' of box are affected by one of the fungal diseases that come under the umbrella of 'blight', and the leaves turn black before dropping. Light trimming back of the dead stems seems to encourage re-growth, so until I am forced to replant the whole thing I tolerate the occasional faded patches, which are at their worst in late winter, though after the wet early summer of 2012 a renewed outbreak occurred in July.

We clip with hand shears (rather than electric trimmers which bruise the foliage and, I reckon, exacerbate the box blight problem) and we do the job on a dry but cloudy day, which allows the cut edges to seal without scorching.

The effect of my sea of box is not quite so dramatic as William Kent's rolling main of laurel, but I enjoy the fluid waves of foliage that flow from the brick-and-flint wall behind it.

A sea of box and a row of conical yew sentinels line the approach to the house (left), and hellebores erupt from the earth below a flowering currant (right).

The chestnut border

The chestnut border (left)
in early spring, awash with
dwarf narcissi and struggling
hellebores. The tree is at its
best in April and May when the
earliest of flowering bulbs, like
hyacinths (below), have faded.

The great conker tree was one of the few features we
inherited when we bought the house, and when I look
at photographs of it from ten years ago I can see that
it has grown considerably larger. Not to worry; it is far
enough away from the house to avoid causing it any kind
of structural damage and I love the horse chestnut as
much as any tree – perhaps more than any when it is in
flower. Every other year I remove a couple of low-arching

branches that threaten to skim the head of anyone walking beneath it.

It sits on a mound of earth around which we built a low retaining wall. The tree's roots still surface in the lawn from time to time, but we tolerate them. Anything planted in the raised bed has to be able to cope with two things: hard, root-riddled earth, and an almost total absence of light in summer when the canopy of the chestnut is in full fig. As a result, spring flowers and bulbs predominate here – dwarf narcissi and erythroniums (dog's tooth violets), *Lilium martagon*, *Anemone blanda* and lily-of-the-valley, coupled with the brightly variegated varieties of euonymus – 'Emerald 'n' Gold' and 'Emerald Gaiety' – which are wonderfully forgiving. When they grow too large and ungainly I go over them with a pair of shears, roughly tidying them up into the shape of low dumplings, and removing any shoots that revert to plain green. *Brunnera macrophylla* and *Tellima grandiflora* are about the only herbaceous perennials that thrive and

spread here, though *Geranium macrorrhizum* would do well. I resist planting it only because I have it in so many other inhospitable spots!

I add to the bulb mixture at planting time each autumn with a few more dwarf narcissi – 'Tête-à-tête' and 'Lemon Silk' do especially well – and enjoy the shafts of sunlight which, in a few weeks' time, will fail to penetrate the leaf canopy. Hyacinths, too, will sputter on from year to year. Lenten hellebores expand only slowly here, and although a sprinkler helps in dry spells, hosepipe bans mean that once established the plants have to be relatively self-sufficient.

But the tree itself is the real star – I watch its fresh green leaves unfurl like starfish outside our bedroom window each April, my head on the pillow. Over the space of three weeks they turn into floppy, half-opened umbrellas before expanding into more rigid Pharaoh's fans, and the house of our next-door neighbours disappears from view. 'The Ts have gone' they tell their children. It is an annual ritual. Then come the candelabras of flower – the moment at which the tree is a thing of majestic beauty.

The current problems of leaf miner and leaf spot do strike as the season progresses, but since the tree is off the main lane of the village, the damage is slower in manifesting itself. London horse chestnuts turn brown by July, the spores of leaf spot being carried by traffic; but trees away from highways and thoroughfares are much less badly blighted.

A nest-box with a camera inside it is fastened to the upper part of the chestnut's trunk, and from my study in the barn I can watch the blue tits rearing their young each spring.

Spring-flowering bulbs are added each autumn at planting time – *Narcissus* 'Thalia' (below) is a favourite.

Buds, shoots and stems

My overriding concern when making the garden was the shape and the layout, but once the basic form was established then the plants themselves had to offer interest – in close-up as well as in combination. I love the variety of leaf shapes, and in spring there is a tremendous sense of renewal as buds burst and leaves unfurl. It is, I suppose, a childish delight to see it all happening, but one that never fades in its intensity.

Some people 'look and never see'. They take in the overall effect but are not concerned with the minute detail. For me these joys are almost equal in the delight they offer, whether it is the soft fur of lamb's ears (*Stachys byzantina*) or the coarseness of rodgersia, or the unfurling croziers of the shuttlecock fern (*Matteuccia struthiopteris*). I am happy to get down on my hands and knees to admire at close quarters the strange flowers of *Arisarum proboscideum*, or gaze into the centre of a perfectly formed camellia, even though I now need a pair of specs to do so.

Within beds and borders the juxtaposing of plants presents the gardener with the greatest of challenges, for they must show each other off – whether by contrasting or blending with one another in terms of form, texture and colour. Achieving satisfying combinations is time consuming and can take several seasons – observing flowering time so that things which coincide can be planted side by side, or noticing leaf and flower combinations which, when planted together, create something, as Sam Goldwyn would have said 'bigger than both of us'.

Height, spread, shape, structure and texture must all be considered, plus the one thing that makes gardening the most difficult art form of all – time. Planting schemes change over the seasons, and they also change over the years in terms of size and scale. A plant combination that has, for several years, been a wonder to behold will suddenly go over the hill and cease to please. That's the time to unpick it and start again.

Above all, I like to grow plants that like me – or, more accurately, my soil and situation. Yes, I like a challenge, but the majority of plants in my garden must enjoy growing there; they must be happy. There is little pleasure to be had in a lifelong struggle – on my part or theirs – even if the plant in question is a treasured rarity. I'd far rather be in the company of something common that grows incredibly well – and so, I suspect, would most gardeners. ❦

Clockwise from top left: the emerging rosette of the foxtail lily (*Eremurus*); fat buds of the wedding cake tree *Cornus controversa* 'Variegata'; useful ground cover from *Lamium* 'White Nancy'; the frilly foliage of *Paeonia tenuifolia*; hosta buds pushing through the earth; the promising flower buds of wisteria at a moment when one prays for lack of frost.

The meadow

The garden itself occupied me most when we first moved here, and the acre and a bit at the back of the long, low barn that ran alongside it – and where I work – was just regularly mown to keep down the nettles and long grass. It was not until we acquired the extra couple of acres five years ago that I sowed a 'proper' wild flower meadow. Until then, I contented myself with planting daffodils in drifts under flowering cherries and crab apples, and planting a few apples and pears (with the intention of making a country orchard with one or two avenues and vistas within it), all of which makes it sound grander than it was.

A great swathe of daffs erupted behind the slope of snowdrops during that first spring, courtesy of the previous owners, and we have added to them over the years, not just with *Crocus tommasinianus*, but with snake's head fritillaries (*Fritillaria meleagris*) and camassias. The snake's heads would prefer slightly damper earth, but they oblige us by returning each April and I plant a few more every autumn.

Statuary needs careful selection. I'd love a massive marble edifice of St George slaying the dragon, to commemorate the day we bought the farmhouse, but I curb my excesses and settle on more appropriate and less expensive ornaments. The statue of Peter Pan is not bronze but a much lighter resin and is modelled on the famous one in Kensington Gardens by Sir George Frampton. I'm not particularly attached to Kensington Gardens but I do like the book of *Peter Pan* by Sir James Barrie and have fond memories of seeing Alastair Sim as Captain Hook at Leeds Grand when I was a nipper. Best of all, I love Frampton's original creation for its elegant lines. A spot at the top of the slope results in the statue being shown off well either against the sloping grass behind it or against a blue or thundery sky, depending on the weather and your angle of view.

A large and rusty pear (left) by Dick Budden – who claims it's really a fig – sits among the daffodils in the meadow, while (right) Peter Pan plays his tune in front of the beehives that border the kitchen garden.

The additional two acres were farmland – well fed with muck and fertilizer for centuries. Now as anybody will tell you, to make a wild flower meadow you need poor land so that the grass does not compete too heavily with the wild flowers and result in their disappearance. I had no option. The ground was rich, over underlying chalk, and well drained. But at least it was bare soil; I did not have the task of killing off the grass before I sowed my wild flower mixture. The meadow comes into its own in summer, but in spring, three years after sowing, the cowslips began to appear, and now they speckle the rough grass profusely and cheer us up for weeks on end in April and May.

The only problem is that they also spring up on the mown 'rides' through the long grass of the meadow, and we then have the heartbreaking job of mowing them and cutting off their flowers. It is a time for clenched teeth, since the prospect of digging each one up by hand and transplanting it would adversely affect my opinion of cowslips. I try not to think of them as the mower rolls on.

Working out where the rides will be mown is fun and agony in equal measure – there are wooden benches at strategic points on the walk around and I like to position them where they offer a good view – either across a sea of wild flowers, or at the end of a long, straight ride where I can pretend I am 'Capability' Brown and borrow the distant landscape. In spite of the size of the meadow, we mow the rides – Bill or Lawrence or me – with a powered rotary mower rather than a ride-on tractor. The finish is so much better and as a child of the parks department I still retain a fondness for stripes – the contrast between the smart rides and the rough meadow pleases me no end.

In the original patch of 'paddock' each spring, we enjoy the snake's heads, the narcissi, the camassias and other bulbs, along with a small grove of flowering cherries. I chose the variety 'Shirotae', which makes an elegant shape and has white blossom faintly tinged with pink. I underplanted each tree with *Narcissus* 'Bell Song', chosen because the trumpets, having opened a pale yellow, fade quickly to soft apricot-pink which complements the cherry blossom. They also flower at the same time. Neat.

Snake's head fritillaries (*Fritillaria meleagris*) erupt across the meadow in April (left), accompanied by a rash of cowslips (*Primula veris*) (above).

'Loveliest of trees,
the cherry now
Is hung with
bloom along
the bough,
And stands about
the woodland ride
Wearing white for
Eastertide.'

A Shropshire Lad
by A.E. Housman

In the meadow, the flowering
cherries, *Prunus* 'Shirotae', are
underplanted with the jonquil
Narcissus 'Bell Song' – the colour
of the narcissus complementing
that of the cherry blossom.

The west garden

We don't really call it that. It's normally referred to as 'over there', with a gesture in its direction, but it is on the west side of the house so it makes sense to give it that label here.

The west garden is the sunniest part of the whole garden, thanks to the conker tree and a 15-foot-high Leyland cypress hedge which border the south side. The hedge

A 'purple and gold' border (below) is at its best in spring when the new foliage is emerging – everything from *Physocarpus opulifolius* 'Dart's Gold' and Bowles's golden grass (*Milium effusum* 'Aureum') to heucheras and berberis, and even a hard-pruned purple-leaved smoke bush (*Cotinus coggygria* 'Royal Purple'). The furniture comes out on to the terrace (right) in a good year while *Pyrus calleryana* 'Chanticleer' is flowering.

was planted by the previous owners to mask the grain silos that used to be there; now the silos have gone but the hedge (trimmed by the redoubtable Gavin each October) screens us from the three houses that replaced them. The west garden is bounded by an old brick-and-flint wall about 5 foot high and, instead of the Leyland hedge and the chestnut tree, a large ash tree erupts on the other side of it and inside the garden grow a pair of ancient yew trees – we are opposite the village church. Surprisingly, although these three giants do screen the sun for part of the day they are not so overpowering as to make the garden shady – the sunlight shines in between them for more of the day than it does not.

When I began to design the garden I started from a terrace we constructed all round the house which we paved with Indian sandstone. I feel guilty about this, ten years on, but York stone was, and is, iniquitously expensive and in short supply. (It will come as a surprise to many – and a relief to most – that there is no decking in my garden. But then the Georgians were not big on decking.)

I started making curved borders on the other side of the lawn from the terrace, but soon found that the shapes did not work. They were flowing and unfussy but somehow not pleasing to the eye. I fell back on the cardinal rule which states that straight lines should come off the formal lines of the house and that curved ones are more appropriate at a distance. So it is that the lawn shapes that surround the house are circular or rectangular, and serpentine paths occur further away. Immediately the effect was much more pleasing. The terrace and the lawns are formal in shape, but the beds and borders I plant in a billowing mass – the informal planting softening the formal geometry. It works for me.

Containers provide portable colour in spring (left), while a Lutyens-style bench (above) has potted hyacinths and a topiary chicken for company.

The barn

The house itself was built between about 1690 and 1777 – we know the latter date precisely since it is carved into several bricks high up on the part of the house known as the 'kitchen extension'. Thanks to the assiduous research of a local historian we know every owner and lessee of this house, and its predecessors, since Domesday. We are the twenty-first family to occupy this patch of Hampshire; the first owner's name, pre Conquest, was Wulfward.

Jane Austen lived in Chawton, just a couple of miles away, the naturalist Gilbert White at nearby Selborne, and we sit on a south-east-facing slope of chalk downland at about 365 feet (111 metres) above sea level.

The house is built of mellow brick with a clay-tiled roof on lower foundations of malmstone – a soft, grey sandstone. The barn alongside it – derelict when we arrived and since restored – is of malmstone with brick quoins (cornerstones).

In here I write and keep my books; it is apart from the house but near enough to pop across and make a cup of tea. It is quiet; peaceful, apart from the plaintive mooing of the cows in the farmyard next door when their calves are taken away.

For the most part I grow plants that thrive here – although we are in southern England this is not the warmest part of the country or county and my daffs are still in bloom well into May in most years. Having chalky soil, rhododendrons are out of the question, though five miles away they thrive on the Surrey greensand. I don't

mind. I don't want them. Rhododendrons do not belong on chalk downland and seem, in this part of the world, to smack of the stockbroker belt.

Camellias are another thing altogether. But they too dislike chalk. So I grow them in tubs of ericaceous compost on the north-east side of the barn and water them with rainwater gathered in water butts positioned at the foot of every downpipe. The received wisdom is that camellias do not enjoy an east-facing position since the early morning sun thaws out their blooms too quickly on frosty mornings. The barn wall is angled sufficiently to the north to prevent this being more than an occasional problem, and so I can drool over my sixteen camellias each spring, feeding them occasionally with dilute liquid sequestrene to maintain the lustre of their leaves.

Camellias behind the barn
(clockwise from top left):
C. x *williamsii* 'Anticipation';
C. x *williamsii* 'E.G. Waterhouse';
the granite-featured Mr Chang
watching over them; C. *japonica*
'Ave Maria'.

Primulas on the grassy bank

Living, as we do, in a country lane, I did not want to make the sloping bank outside the house too smart, too prinked, and so I stuck with the existing native wild flowers and let them proliferate. Country verges that boast daisies and speedwell are always more appealing to me than those that are inappropriately manicured, almost as if they were staking a claim on urban civilisation. I prefer my country verges wild and woolly. Visits to Devon and Cornwall where the towering hedge-banks are every bit as colourful as a domestic herbaceous border can keep me botanising happily for hours.

On our more modest Hampshire bank, with its chalky subsoil, the primroses (*Primula vulgaris*) self-seed each year and the red valerian (*Centranthus ruber*) does the same at the foot of the wall. I have tried to get dwarf narcissi growing here, but the fiercely draining earth, combined with the rain-shadow effects of the flint wall, does not offer them enough sustenance. Snowdrops fare rather better – I added to the few that already sprang up here and the plantation continues to expand.

From May onwards we cut the grass on either side of the gates so that it remains shorter, but not exactly to what you might call bowling-green standard. Outside the rest of the garden wall the bank grows unrestrained – a mixture of cow parsley (*Anthriscus sylvestris*) and goat's rue (*Galega officinalis*), marguerites (*Leucanthemum vulgare*) and all kinds of grasses. We strim it off at the end of summer to allow the walkers along The Pilgrim's Way – a route that passes our garden – an easier passage. I hear them, over the garden wall, as I work among the plants – their footsteps and murmuring voices a wistful reminder of the centuries through which this unassuming and meandering pathway has accommodated travellers journeying from Winchester to Canterbury. Though I doubt whether today many of them make it as far as the seat of Christianity, the better part of a hundred miles away. Some of these walkers are of mature years – 'The Evergreens' – whose journey will end with a pub lunch; others are schoolchildren out on a ramble. They are happy sounds to hear on a spring afternoon, though I wonder if they notice the primroses …

Red valerian (left) skirts the old garden wall and sometimes even seeds itself among the flints, while primroses (right) open their first flowers at any time from January to March, depending on the weather.

The greenhouse borders

I built my first greenhouse when I was ten years old. It was made from lumps of wood salvaged from my parents' old double bed, and bits of timber brought home by my dad from work (he was a plumber but seemed to have access to old floorboards and offcuts as a part of his daily life). With a sheet of polythene from the local ironmongers I was able to construct (with the aid of a hammer, nails and drawing pins) a 6 foot by 3 foot structure that was home to geraniums and spider plants, a false castor oil palm and two pet mice. Bliss! My present structure is smarter in appearance but the pleasure remains the same.

Over the years I've had aluminium alloy and western red cedar greenhouses of various sizes, but the newer kinds of glasshouse, made of powder-coated alloy, are, I think, the best. They look decorative (especially in a more traditional garden like mine) and, most importantly, they need very little maintenance other than an annual wash-down to remove grime. Gone are the days of re-painting to produce a greenhouse with pristine white glazing bars – now it can be achieved once and for all in the factory.

The lily-flowered tulip 'White Triumphator' takes some beating when it comes to classic looks and durability.

Mine sits just across the drive from the kitchen window – angled so that it faces directly towards us – and the stone-flagged path that leads to it is flanked by 3-foot-wide borders that are the only parts of the garden to sport spring and summer bedding.

The circular bed halfway up the path was home to a wonderful old apple tree – awash in spring with pink and white blossom that looked like coconut ice. Alas, half the tree was felled by high winds a few years ago and it had to be removed. But what to put in its place? I considered another tree, but getting it established in a spot occupied by an old-established apple would have meant digging out and replacing a lot of soil. I settled, instead, on a circular water sculpture by Allison Armour-Wilson. I'd first seen it at the Chelsea Flower Show and thought it a handsome thing – not fussy and twiddly as so many 'water features' are. The stainless-steel dish supports a

transparent, water-filled acrylic sphere over which the ripples fall silently. It sparkles in sunshine and shimmers even in cloudy weather. But there is one problem – after a few sunny days the water goes green. We experimented for weeks with assorted potions, finally discovering a regime of chlorine tablets that achieved lasting clarity, without affecting the birdlife that visits it. To my chagrin 'birdlife' includes the ducks and moorhens who perversely prefer it for their morning ablutions to the wildlife pond that was especially constructed for them behind the barn. I suppose that to them it represents a kind of discreet *en suite* arrangement. The whole thing has to be emptied and cleaned out once a fortnight thanks to their daily deposits, but that's the thing about wildlife – you can't choose it; it chooses you …

Quince trees of the variety 'Meech's Prolific' were planted at the four path corners, and are being trained into giant lollipops. Each October the beds themselves are planted up with tulips – the colour scheme being varied from year to year – and each spring I wait for the green spears to push up through the dark earth; the anticipation of flowering is almost as enjoyable as the event itself.

I love tulips; they have such elegant form and, weather permitting, will last for several weeks in full bloom before they go over. The lily-flowered varieties, opening in late April or early May are a particular favourite – tall and well proportioned but sturdy enough to withstand strong winds. When they are over I dig them up and hand them over to a friend for his garden, but only because I feel the need to try a different variety each year. That said, nothing really surpasses the pristine beauty of 'White Triumphator'. It is, without doubt, a class act.

Tulips 'Pink Diamond' and 'Queen of Night' (left) make a pleasing combination, while a lead pig (below) ambles past the variety 'China Pink' (also on page 41).

Tulips in the grass

Mown rides through rough grass I have always found attractive, and they can make an otherwise neglected area look more 'in hand'. It is the contrast between the finely mown pathways and the rough grass that appeals – especially cheering when the longer grass is planted up with bulbs.

Through the meadow area at the back of the barn I have mown three straight rides that are bordered by avenues of beech, lime and flowering cherry. The cherries have replaced flowering crab apples (malus) that just about survived but did nothing like so well as the cherries, which love the underlying chalk (as do most stone fruit). With all plants I am patient in their early years; giving them a chance to get their roots down and thrive. But there comes a point where one has to throw in the trowel and admit defeat – as was the case with the crab apples.

In the far wild flower meadow (sorry, I don't mean to sound grand) I have stuck to native wild flowers, so, when it comes to bulbs, only snake's head fritillaries are allowed to join them, and snowdrops under the trees. But in the section nearer the barn I have planted daffodils and narcissi, camassias and tulips. The latter I planted with hesitation. Tulips I love in beds and borders, but when they are naturalised in grass I am always a little uneasy. They often look too 'cultivated'; too formal and robust. However, I chose three varieties whose colour I thought would complement the blossom of the crab apples – the light purple–violet 'Attila', softer pink 'Gabriella' and deep purple 'Negrita'. The result was, I think, successful – especially on a bright and sunny day when this patch of meadow seemed to glow.

But not all tulips are happy to flower every year, especially when they are grown in grass, and so it proved, with 'Negrita' doing well in the second year and 'Attila' and 'Gabriella' putting in a poor show. I suspected, at the outset, that I would have to plant new bulbs each autumn, and that is what I shall now do.

The Prince of Wales has added *Allium* 'Purple Sensation' to part of his wild flower meadow at Highgrove. I may pluck up the courage later …

One crab apple that did do well on our soil was *Malus* 'Evereste' and that, along with the two white-flowered beauties *Malus transitoria* and *Malus hupehensis,* has been allowed to stay. In April and May this patch of flower-filled meadow would make even the most cynical gardener smile. 🌱

Malus 'Evereste' (left) growing among the tulip-filled grass. Deep purple 'Negrita' (below), pale pink 'Gabriella' and violet–purple 'Attila' tulips.

The summerhouse border

This only became the summerhouse border a couple of years ago when, irritated that it was too cold to sit in the garden on a sunny spring day, we invested in a small, hexagonal summerhouse and plonked it among the flowers. (Well, I say plonked, but the foundations were quite substantial.) The shelter it provides – often with the doors wide open – is enough to extend the garden's entertainment possibilities – without the wind at your back the garden can feel two coats warmer. It sits in one of the deeper borders which is planted up in my usual fashion – a mixture of shrubs, shrub roses, border perennials and bulbs with clematis growing up through rusted iron obelisks. I am not good at sitting down in the garden, but comfortably cushioned garden furniture inside the summerhouse is gradually persuading me otherwise.

Three shallow steps lead up to it and I splashed out and got a local joiner to make me some oak railings whose finials match the shape of two clipped box sentinels further along the border. I don't suppose anyone else notices but it pleases me …

I don't go in for the 'dig up and divide everything every three years' method of gardening. If something is doing well I leave it alone and only disturb it when it starts to look tired. As a result, my beds and borders tend to evolve for ten years or so – the contents being rejuvenated or replaced piecemeal – and then I might have a blitz and start again, but only when I'm weary of the outlook.

Nic Fiddian Green's 'Mighty Head' (left) stands in the centre of a round lawn backed by foliage. The elegant, pendulous flowers of *Lamprocapnos spectabilis* (*Dicentra*) luxuriate in the shade (right).

Before planting we dig and manure the ground and give it a generous dressing of blood, fish and bonemeal – my general-purpose fertilizer that seems to be a panacea for all ills. I have never double-dug ground except for an examination, and that was more than forty years ago! Nowadays I doubt that my back would cope with it.

I tend to plant quite thickly – placing plants a sufficient distance apart to allow them to cover the ground within their first year. Soil is not a pretty commodity, and I really don't want to have to look at it for longer than I am forced. Shrubs, naturally, have to be given room to grow outwards over several years, and so I plant annuals or perennials between them that can be removed when the shrub expands. After planting I sometimes mulch with chipped bark, but not always. A two-inch layer does have the advantage of sealing in moisture and keeping down weeds, but it also gets chucked about every morning by blackbirds. Thanks to our organic way of life and copious feeding we have a lot of blackbirds. I use a rubber-toothed rake most days to sweep the bark from the lawn back on to the border. As I say, I *sometimes* mulch with chipped bark …

The whole feel of the garden here is on what I'd call the 'classical' side of cottage gardening; so instead of using rustic poles – which are a bit lumpen and cumbersome – I prefer the cleaner lines of rusted iron. It is of this material that my obelisks are made. Having enquired about them of a rather chic supplier at the Chelsea Flower Show one year and been horrified at the price, I found a local blacksmith who was prepared to make them for me, along with 4-, 5- and 6-foot steel stakes with round balls on top. They came out at a fraction of the 'designer' price and will last for donkey's years. What's more, they don't poke your eye out when you are pushing them into the ground.

In spring I enjoy the self-seeded primroses, dwarf irises and the emerging foliage and locket-shaped flowers of *Lamprocapnos spectabilis* – the bleeding heart or lady in the bath (hold each flower upside down and you will see her sitting there, wearing a bath cap). She'll be followed by aquilegias, astrantias and peonies, before the border really gets into its stride in summer.

Spring shows up the gaps, and it's in April and May that I look around for spaces to squeeze in another plant or two that I haven't grown before, though I have to confess that there is a great temptation to fall back on hardy geraniums and penstemons – both of which are the greatest ground-rent payers in any garden. Without *Geranium phaeum* and *G. macrorrhizum* in all their various forms my garden would be a poorer place in spring.

The flowers of *Viburnum carlesii* 'Aurora' (left) have the most heavenly scent. The signpost will be familiar to all Beatrix Potter lovers, but you have to guess which book … The summerhouse (below) becomes more submerged by flowers as the season progresses.

The dolphin pond

At some time in the fifteenth century, the Italian sculptor Andrea del Verrocchio created a sculpture of a boy and a dolphin. A copy of it graces The Queen's Garden at Kew, where I used to work, and that is my excuse for having a much cheaper copy of it in a round, raised stone pond in a circular lawn at one 'end' of the garden. Oh, I know it might look a bit old-fashioned, but it reminds me of five happy years at Kew and the elegant garden created behind Kew Palace where that much-maligned monarch George III lived.

The fountain comes on every morning at seven, courtesy of a time switch, and goes off at 10.30pm because it sits below our bedroom window and Mrs T says the sound of running water keeps her awake. I say that it's a good job we didn't buy a water mill, but before I get very far with the argument she's dropped off …

A heron filched all the goldfish I put in it, so now it boasts just three miniature water lilies and a collar of clipped box to soften the effect of the raised stone sides.

The garden that surrounds it is planted up predominantly with white- and blue-flowered plants – 'Spring Green' tulips and 'Thalia' narcissi are among the first to appear, along with white self-seeded forget-me-nots, white dicentras and blue pulmonaria.

White tulips and narcissi and a weeping silver-leaved pear (*Pyrus salicifolia* 'Pendula') make a spring backdrop to the dolphin pond.

The delphinium border

Until we came here I'd never grown decent delphiniums. The stoney, chalky soil at Barleywood was not much to their liking, although they were extraordinarily appreciated by slugs and snails who whipped them off at ground level with all the precision of a bacon slicer. But when we made this circular garden with the dolphin pond at its centre we created two tiered raised beds on one side to cater for the slope in the ground that bridged the gap between the stone barn and the garden itself. It meant that we had to import some soil. I plumped for a sandy loam (who wouldn't?) and worked in plenty of well-rotted manure.

Never having had much luck before, I decided that this was 'do or die' as far as delphiniums were concerned, and so I scrutinised Messrs Blackmore & Langdon's stand at the Chelsea Flower Show and ordered three plants each of half a dozen varieties that took my eye to give them a try. The blue and white 'Delft' theme was established.

From year one the plants simply took off and, astonishingly for a garden on chalk where snails thrive, the plants are seldom troubled by them. My only explanation is that the soil is so hospitable to the delphiniums that they grow fast enough to be out of the snails' way before they have time to do much damage, and, indeed, the stems are a good 3 feet high by the end of April. At that time in a cool spring most hostas – which do show evidence of slug and snail damage – are only just beginning to unfurl and are more easily reached and shredded.

The garden is entered via a small flight of steps and I could not resist flanking them with ball finials on top of the piers at either end of the knapped flint walls. Small box-edged beds, each with a fastigiate hornbeam in the centre, add to the classical formality. I did warn you …

The delphinium border in spring (left) and the entrance to the dolphin pond garden (right) – the tulips have since been replaced by box balls in gravel.

The dolphin pond through the seasons

Seasonal changes are, for me, the greatest pleasure of British gardens, and the challenge is to create a garden which, while it may look different at each season, nevertheless has something of interest all the year round. I can see the dolphin pond garden from the barn where I work. In late spring (main picture), early spring (top right), early summer (centre) and winter (bottom) – in this case covered by snow – there is always something to enjoy. Thanks to my love of topiary – formally clipped yew and box in particular – the garden has shape and form even in the depths of winter.

Summer

Summer sun
turns the meadow
grasses gold,
while the bees
buzz among
scabious and
knapweed, bird's-
foot trefoil and
wild carrot ...

———

Introduction

Quite when spring turns into summer I am not sure. The calendar says that it is the middle of June, but in some years it sneaks in earlier, departs for a while and then – hopefully – returns. For me, summer begins when I return home from seven days at the Chelsea Flower Show during the third week in May, and, like most who go there, I come back experiencing a mixture of emotions – eagerness to see what has happened while I have been away (late May is usually a time of rapid growth and development) and anxiety when comparing my own efforts to those of the masters of garden design and plant cultivation.

I tell myself, year after year, that Chelsea is not real; that it is a pastiche; smoke and mirrors. And yet, there is that little niggle at the back of my mind which says that although the glimpses of paradise created in those model gardens in the grounds of the Royal Hospital are transient and artificial, they were, for that brief, shining moment, fragments of perfection. Could the same be achieved in the longer term? At least the show keeps me on my toes, and after a few days have passed, the unease settles into realism and I content myself with continuing in my quest for perfection, knowing that it cannot really be achieved.

I've always regarded myself as a gardener who designs a bit, rather than a garden designer proper. I was *taught* landscape design and construction at Kew by some of the best in the business, but somehow the fact that I started life as a grower of plants rather than an artist (my one 'O' level in art apart) I feel unable to fully commit to that state of mind. And I do think it is a state of mind.

I listen to my Chelsea Flower Show colleagues – Joe Swift and Andy Sturgeon, Cleve West and Tom Stuart-Smith – waxing lyrical about garden design in terms that seem at best esoteric and at worst a tad pretentious, and explaining why so-and-so's garden is so much better than whatshisname's. All too often it is whatshisname's garden that I prefer and I frequently discover that whatshisname is a gardener first and a designer second. Although I love more than anything putting a garden together, I can't really sympathise with the perceived elitism of garden design. Sometimes it seems to me to be just too artful and self-aware. For me, the best gardens are those that it is a delight to be in rather than to look at; gardens where the design is subservient to the planting.

Somewhere for lunch, or supper, in summer – a table and chairs among the flowers on the west-facing terrace of the house.

It's for this reason that my garden has plenty of sitting places; places from which to look and, hopefully, be calmed, or inspired. Not that I sit down as much as I should. I'm working at it; telling myself that it would be better for my health if I paused for ten minutes rather than ten seconds. But there is always a weed to be pulled up, or a flower to examine. Only when we eat or have a cup of tea or coffee outdoors will I pause for as long as it takes to consume. Though, to be fair, I can stop when I'm eating – the consumption of food being a pleasure equivalent to that of gardening. To sit at a table among the flowers, gazing down a vista, or at a well-planted bed or border, is one of life's greatest joys, even if I do make mental notes about how things could be improved.

Success, they say, is a journey, not a destination, and the same is true of gardening. It's not that I am discontented, simply that the quest for unattainable perfection continues; it is one of the greatest pleasures in gardening. Still, in summer, I do tell myself that this is the season of fulfilment, when any garden worth its salt is at its best, and that if I cannot sit back and enjoy my garden now, there is something sadly amiss. So I do. Even if, every now and again, there is just the faintest niggle that something could be just that little bit better ...

It's worth allowing *Papaver somniferum* (left) to seed around simply for its ability to attract hoverflies. Steamer chairs by the wildlife pond (right) offer a ringside view of bird, insect and fish activity.

Silver birch border

The 6-foot-deep border at the foot of the Leyland cypress hedge faces north-west, and so does not receive any direct sunlight until mid-afternoon in summer, and hardly any when the sun is lower during autumn and winter. It is not directly up against the hedge – I allowed a 4-foot-wide grass path between them, for access and to ensure the border was eased out into the light as much as possible and sufficiently distant from the dense root system of the conifer to avoid it being sucked dry of moisture. Leyland cypress has had a bad press, but if close-clipped just once a year – in late summer or early autumn, taking care not to cut into brown foliage – it makes a good, dense, green hedge that is crisp of line for six months of the year and a perfect background to perennials and shrubs. On its own it can be oppressive, but if its dusky foliage is regarded as a backdrop, you can make the most if its virtues.

To lighten up the view I planted three evenly spaced trios of *Betula utilis* var. *jacquemontii* along its length, and after ten years they are about 20 feet high – just beginning to peep over the top of the 18-foot-high hedge. If I were to plant them again I would choose *Betula albosinensis* 'Fascination', since its bark is even creamier and the young stems have a rufous colouring which contrasts wonderfully with the paler bark of the trunk.

In the two gaps between the birches sit classical stone urns – they seem to suit my idea of a Georgian garden, though they are modern, not antique. The planting itself has just been changed from a mixture of shrubs and perennials that were mainly pink and purple, to a scheme of purple and gold. Time will tell whether or not *Choisya* 'Sundance' is as happy to grow here as the variegated

weigela. One thing that does enjoy life here is Solomon's seal – *Polygonatum* x *hybridum*, which has almost turned into a weed, along with the equally happy Miss Willmott's ghost – *Eryngium giganteum*. But I hoik out those I do not want each year and their progeny continue to thrive. Hardy geraniums are a godsend. Along the back of the border is a row of around 25 different hostas – the nearest I get to stamp collecting. Once established they are remarkably tolerant of what can be a rain shadow area.

The hedge itself (originally planted to mask farm silos, and now neighbouring houses) began to suffer in January a few years ago – areas of dark brown began to spread. I endeavoured to work out what might be the problem. Fungal disease? No sign. Pest attack? No. I examined the soil below the hedge and discovered it was bone dry – in the dead of winter. We ran a trickle hose along the bottom of the hedge and turned on the tap for a few hours each day. The hedge slowly came back to life.

So if you have a conifer hedge that is tall and thick, do keep an eye on it for water; if your soil is on the light side it may be thirsty – even in winter. Ours, I'm relieved to say, has made a full recovery, and a single clipping over in September or October maintains its density and its crisp outline. I don't do the job; that's the province of Gavin, our agile tree surgeon, who is happier with a powered hedge trimmer 20 feet up in the air than I am.

Silver birches stand out well against the Leyland cypress hedge (left).

Wisteria on the barn

Wisteria grew up the front of the house when we arrived – one plant on each side of the front door – but both were on their last legs. I bit the bullet and replaced them. I wished I had not. The replacement plants were not keen on our alkaline soil and perhaps the borders in which they grew were tired of wisteria. It is seldom a good idea to replace like with like. I cosseted them for a few years and then gave up and had them out. Their reluctance

to flower, coupled with the infelicity of their chlorotic yellow foliage against the mellow orange brick was not a joy to behold. We have replaced them with roses.

The wisteria that grows by the barn is in far better heart and its colouring in both leaf and flower suits the pale malmstone. I cannot claim credit for its generous performance year on year. Its roots delve beneath the paving where they benefit from a cool, moist run, and that alone is responsible for the plant's success.

What the wisteria does enjoy, though, is full sunshine, and since the side of the barn that it decorates faces south-west, the stems are well ripened. I prune it twice a year – once in July, shortening those unwanted, snaking stems to about a foot long, and again in January when all sideshoots are cut back to finger length.

Along the front of the barn (the camellias are grown on the shady north-eastern side) are large pots of lavender – mainly English of the variety 'Hidcote', with the odd pot of French thrown in. They enjoy the summer baking, and anyone walking down the path can brush against them and enjoy the mentho-lyptus aroma of their foliage. Two potted box bushes clipped into spirals flank a terracotta head and a plaster plaque at the axis of the barn and the house paths. We do a lot of watering in summer!

French lavender in terracotta pots (left), sits alongside English lavender. The wisteria winds around an oak beam (right) and releases a wonderful perfume on May evenings.

The wildlife pond

The area of rough grass and nettles behind the barn comprised about an acre and a quarter when we bought the house; it seemed a bit featureless and I needed to find a way of attracting more wildlife. A pond was the obvious solution, but the ground slopes gently there so we had to create a 'bund' – a raised bank of imported topsoil – to achieve a level surface. We built and consolidated this and excavated a crater (ponds always look like lunar craters before they are filled – it is a worrying time) and took advice on the best lining. We settled on thick, fibrous pond underlay, a layer of stout butyl, another of underlay, then 3 inches of soil before filling with a hosepipe. It ran for nearly three days (there was no hosepipe ban).

The layers of underlay and butyl make sure that even if a deer or a stray cow from the farm ambled into the water the lining would not be damaged. The soil layer allowed for the rooting of submerged aquatics – water milfoil and water crowfoot in preference to invasive Canadian pondweed. But some of the latter did manage to find its way in, and each summer we have a thinning out session when we think it will cause the least disturbance.

The marginal aquatics planted on the pond's banks play host to damselflies and dragonflies in summer; frogs and toads, newts and a shoal of roach have all made a home here, and mallards and moorhens breed every year. We provided the facilities; they came of their own accord. It is one of the best things we have ever done.

In summer, a seat offers views of swallows skimming the surface and moorhen chicks racing across lily pads.

The summerhouse border

This border is an example of how a garden develops with use. There are some bits which, while being perfectly pleasant, just never quite 'gel', and we had decided that we wanted somewhere to sit, out of the wind. This corner – seen on the previous pages before the summerhouse was erected in September 2010 – was the chosen spot. We have never regretted it. It may seem to be overstating the case to say that it has changed our lives, but what it has done is enabled us to sit in the garden, to have a cup of tea, or a snack, or a full-blown meal, when otherwise it would be just too chilly. The doors are usually left open but the shelter itself is enough to make the temperature a little warmer, and there is a small electric heater to take the nip out of the air on winter days.

I am beginning to sound like an old-age pensioner. Well, what the heck! But to sit there with the Sunday papers, among the flowers, is a weekend delight, and I would not have believed just how much use we have got out of it.

I wanted a building that was reasonably handsome and which would suit the nature and style of the garden. The hexagonal structure, with its shingle roof (I'm not a fan of thatch, except where it fits into the local vernacular) fitted the bill perfectly, and the woodwork is painted to match the other structures in the garden.

The oak fences that lead up to it were made to my design by a local joiner. They were a bit of an extravagance, but they do look neat. 🌱

The summerhouse border before the summerhouse (previous page and left). Looking as though it has always been there (below), the summerhouse sits among a mixture of shrubs and border perennials.

The big border

It's not that big, just fairly deep, separating the 'house lawns' from the winding grass path at the back of the garden which runs alongside the winter border. Being deep, I've planted a 'spine' of shrubs – philadelphus, osmanthus, shrub roses, a black cut-leaved elder and the wedding cake tree, *Cornus controversa* 'Variegata', down the centre. In so doing I've created a double-aspect border that is purple and gold on one side of the spine and a mixture of pinks and whites and mauves on the other (instead of one consistent planting scheme throughout).

I've become rather weary of the current garden design fashion for taking twenty or more plants of six species and mixing them all together to make a haze of indistinct colour. It was fun when it was novel – ten years ago – but now it seems cowardly, non-committal and hackneyed. I'd rather plant in pleasing-shaped drifts using the old 'threes, fives and sevens' technique. In reality, the oddness of the numbers matters not a jot; when you get past five, who's counting? But there is far more fun, excitement and risk in being decisive; in placing one drift against another and seeing how it fares with its neighbours. We all worry whether a scheme will work or not, but we need to remind ourselves (every year in my case) that if it doesn't work it can be dug up and moved the following year.

Eremurus and oriental poppies enjoy the sunny spot and well-drained soil in front of the wedding cake tree, *Cornus controversa* 'Variegata'.

The winter garden in summer

The winding grass path farthest from the house snakes between 'the big border' and a narrower one which sits alongside the brick-and-flint wall that is our boundary. I call it 'the winter garden' because it is planted with umpteen clumps of miniature narcissi which come into their own when the leafless tree canopy allows in more light than in summer. In winter it draws me away from the house, and in early summer the dying foliage is not so 'up front' to be a nuisance. But in May and early June the border takes on a completely different feel when Japanese maples come into leaf alongside the wall, and purple- and gold-leaved plants burst their buds opposite. Overhanging the path is an established laburnum, and for a couple of weeks in early summer it frames the view elegantly.

I love laburnums. The childhood warnings about their poisonous seeds have put a lot of folk off them and, to be fair, their flowering season is short. But if the variety *Laburnum* x *watereri* 'Vossii' is chosen, it does not produce seeds, and although all other parts of the plant are toxic it is unlikely that any child would choose to nibble them.

The shortness of its season cannot be alleviated, but it is so glorious and so eagerly anticipated that I'm prepared to give the one tree house-room. I toy with creating a laburnum tunnel as did Rosemary Verey at Barnsley House in Gloucestershire, and which I also tended in The Queen's Garden at Kew, but space, and the dullness of the tunnel for eleven months of the year, make me stay my hand and settle for the single specimen. Fleeting moments of pleasure in a garden are often appreciated far more than those which last for months and whose familiarity, however spectacular, begins to pall. 🌱

The solitary laburnum tree (left) dangles its flowers over a winding grass path in early summer, framing a Lutyens-style bench at the end.

Ferns carpet the ground (below) as the shade deepens under an old yew tree, and tree ferns push up among them.

I never tire of
mowing; it is
thinking time,
looking time.
A time of just
being in my
garden and
endeavouring to
exercise some
kind of control
over it ...

———

The west garden

My tastes have changed over the years. Our first garden,
just 15 feet by 35 feet behind an end-of-terrace cottage, was
informal, cut in half by a small pool with a plank bridge,
with curving borders on either side and a greenhouse at
the bottom. As I have grown older I have come to value
the sense of order, perspective and cleanliness of line
that a formal garden offers, while still retaining a love of
generous informality between those constraining shapes

Humphry Repton (below) casts
a critical eye over the garden.
Allium 'Globemaster' (right)
explodes above the leaves
of persicaria.

(which is a rather pompous way of saying that I appreciate straight lines more than I used to).

The garden on the west side of the house is the most formal of all, with a small parterre of clipped, dwarf box between the terrace and the lawn. For several years I planted up the parterre with tulips for spring, and cosmos, osteospermums or zinnias for summer colour. But it never quite worked – the flowers flopping over the low hedge, masking its shape. I resorted, instead, to box balls surrounded by pea shingle. It was much more crisp, if unadventurous, but needed a centrepiece. First it was a large pot; then an urn; and then I saw a terracotta statue of Mozart that the potter Jim Keeling had made, so I asked him if he could make me one of Humphry Repton (1752–1818) – the man who, following Lancelot 'Capability' Brown's natural landscape movement, brought the garden up to the house once more. Now Humphry presides over a view that I hope would meet his approval, and his proprietorial pose makes me smile.

House walls

The farmhouse we live in was built bit by bit. The cellar is thought to be Elizabethan, the oldest part of the house above it dates from about 1690, and the majority from the early 1700s. The 'new' kitchen extension dates from 1777; we know that because the builders had the foresight to carve their initials into the bricks along with the date.

Originally a 'hall-house' (there are blackened beams in the attic), it was villa-ified in the late eighteenth century. That explains the 'join' that is plainly visible on the south front of the house – the right-hand side is older than the left. The Georgian renovations produced a house of five bays which has a classic doll's-house symmetry and looks as though one side of it ought to be hinged so that the front can be opened and the furniture re-arranged.

Roses now grow up the walls, having replaced the ailing wisteria. 'Madame Alfred Carrière' was already here and continues to thrive, and I have added 'Ayrshire Splendens', 'New Dawn', and a clutch of pink David Austin roses – A Shropshire Lad, 'Constance Spry', Mortimer Sackler and, best of all, The Generous Gardener, which has disease-resistant foliage as well as repeat flushes of flower.

Never willing to settle for one plant when I can accommodate two, I have trained clematis up many of the climbing roses. Not the large-flowered kinds, or the rampant *C. montana*, but the smaller-flowered Viticella hybrids, such as the purple 'Polish Spirit', which flower profusely in early summer and which can be cut back hard to ground level in early winter, thus relieving the roses (and my critical eye) of a mass of dead foliage and stems. Up they spring each February with fresh growth that is soon smothered in flower.

North walls are less conducive to the establishment of climbers, but here the climbing hydrangea, *Hydrangea petiolaris* does its bit, even if it does take a few years to settle in and bloom reliably each May. But the flowers, to me, are secondary, since I love the contrast of its fleshy lime-green leaves with the dusky orange of the dry brickwork. A lathering of manure water over the wall encourages the stems to cling on with their aerial roots if they are reluctant to grip. The smell does not last long.

The pink-dipped leaves of *Actinidia kolomikta* (left) mix wonderfully well with the flowers of the rose 'Constance Spry' trained up the house wall.

The wisteria (right) has since been replaced by roses; *Pyrus* 'Chanticleer' erupts through a square spat of clipped box.

The rose arbour

When we moved house, ten years ago, I dug up and removed very few plants. It would have been like selling a painting and cutting out and keeping a few bits that were particularly special to me. It's not that I am making great claims for my artistry in garden-making, just that I didn't want to leave behind a garden full of holes. It didn't seem right. But I did take one or two large pots filled with topiary, and a rusted iron arbour.

It's funny how tastes change; my dad would have given anything rusty a good coat of Hammerite to preserve it. Rusted ironwork (as opposed to 'rusty' – the folk who sell these artefacts are very particular about that) is now hugely fashionable and, I have to say, I'm very fond of the comfortable appearance of rust in the garden. It reminds me of my grandfather's allotment.

But where to put my arbour? I settled on a spot in the middle of 'the big border', which is an axis and a focal point at the end of the terrace running along the south side – the 'front' – of the house. The area beneath it was paved, a path constructed to get to it and a wooden chair settled inside it. Two roses were trained over the framework: the vigorous, egg-yolk yellow 'Alchymist' (1956), and the older 'Albéric Barbier' (1900). I tie in the stems I can reach, and every four or five years I have a blitz and chop both of them back so that the elegant proportions of the ironwork can still be seen (otherwise I might just as well have a thicket of briars).

Elsewhere in the garden, roses push up among other shrubs and border perennials. I can never have too many of them. Almost always they are shrub roses –

either ancient ones with history but only one season of flowering – or modern ones that have the advantage of repeat flowering. And scent; always scent. A rose without scent is like a kiss without a squeeze. 🌱

Clockwise from top left: *Rosa* 'Complicata' (date unknown); The Pilgrim (1991); 'Celsiana' (1750); 'Baronne Prévost' (1842). The rose arbour (above) swamped under the flowers of 'Albéric Barbier' and 'Alchymist' in June.

The delphinium border

They are martyrs to slugs. And snails. And our chalky soil helps snails make sturdy shells. But I have always loved the plants that are the mollusc equivalent of caviar. Blackmore & Langdon's exhibits have made gardeners drool at the Chelsea Flower Show for a century. I wanted to grow delphiniums of comparable stature.

We built a raised bed at one end of the circular garden. It was filled with sandy loam (when bringing in soil you might as well import stuff that is easy to cultivate). I planted my blue and white delphiniums in groups of three. They thrived. There are several reasons, I think: slugs and snails are less of a problem on well-drained soil. Delphiniums grow quickly through the early stages of emerging from the ground (the time when they are most susceptible to being nibbled) on lighter, sun-warmed earth. But they also need plenty of food, and we worked in well-rotted manure and compost before planting. In damp springs rigid copper collars encircle the emerging shoots to protect them until the danger of their being shorn off at ground level by marauding molluscs is past.

Staking must be undertaken before the stems are too tall or the moment is missed and they topple. We use 6-foot-tall, rusted-iron, bobble-topped stakes, which are pushed among the plants when they are a foot high, then linked with soft twine – ever higher as the stems extend.

The plants' only failing is their unglamorous 'legs', since the leaves at the base of the stems turn brown at the merest hint of a water shortage. The answer is to plant a tallish geranium such as 'Mrs Kendall Clark' at their base to hide any shortcomings. It seems to do the trick. 🌱

West garden poppies

Oriental poppies seem to do well with us on our free-draining alkaline soil. They need little encouragement, with their fat tap-roots, which can be chopped up and used as root cuttings. Once planted, the clumps expand year on year and in late May and early June the plump, roughly hairy buds pop open and the tissue-paper flowers seem to inflate by the hour and turn into goblets of the richest colours. The display lasts for several weeks.

'Patty's Plum' (below) opening her flowers in early June. Pots of hostas (right) flank the three steps that lead down into the west garden.

Providing the first flush of growth with circular wire supports raised a foot above ground really is worthwhile. This prevents the plants flopping, and if positioned when the stems are 9 inches high, they soon provide an invisible support, rather like a botanical corset. Tying them up once they have flopped is a recipe for disaster.

'Patty's Plum', allegedly found growing on a compost heap, is a wonderful shade of pale, dusky lilac–purple, and 'Lauren's Lilac' is similar. Sandy Worth, who runs Water Meadow Nursery at nearby Cheriton, grows the new race of so-called super-poppies derived from *Papaver orientale*, and I have acquired a few from her, including the rich red 'Heartbeat'. Older favourites include 'Black and White' and 'Mrs Perry', a warm shade of pink.

The poppies grow better than I deserve, since when they fade I scissor off stems and tatty leaves at ground level and they soon send up fresh foliage that seems equally efficient at feeding the roots and ensuring their survival.

Croquet on the lawn

To call the game we play 'croquet' is a bit of a nerve.
We take it in turns to knock balls through the hoops but
our knowledge of the finer points of the game is worse
than slight. I'm not even sure that we start in the right
place. One day I will sit down and read the rule book and
then Hurlingham will tremble. But even in our sporting
ignorance, summer evenings are fun, with a glass or two
of wine and the sound of hilarity ringing out on the calm
evening air.

The gazebo is somewhere to flop and admire or criticize
the sporting prowess of opponents. It catches the
westering sun, and makes the point that it is always
a good idea to work out the orientation of the garden
before installing any features – be it a greenhouse or a
washing line, a patio or a pond. Those who want to relax
in the late rays of the sun when returning home from
work in the summer would do well not to site their sitting
area on the eastern side of the house. Obvious, I know,
but so often overlooked in the race to 'do the garden'.

The gazebo catches the last rays
of the early evening sun, offering
a welcome pick-me-up before
it dips behind the farmer's barn
next door. Gazebo + glass of
wine + evening sunshine = swift
summer unwind.

The greenhouse

While my tastes have changed over the years in terms of garden design, I fear I might be stuck in a rut when it comes to my greenhouse arrangements. Had you walked inside my first model, fifty years ago, you would have seen a mixture of pelargoniums and fuchsias, spider plants and succulents, begonias and salpiglossis with a few seed-raised coleus grown for their coloured leaves. If you walk inside my, admittedly, slightly larger structure today you will see a mixture of pelargoniums, fuchsias, begonias, succulents and salpiglossis, with a few seed-raised coleus grown for their coloured leaves. Where the spider plants have gone I know not; they must just have dwindled out of my consciousness. The reason is simple – I love my greenhouse to be filled with summer colour, and the prospect of a tropical-sized heating bill in winter is one I regard as a needless extravagance. The greenhouse is heated sufficiently to keep out the frost and keep rooted cuttings of pelargoniums alive, but that is about all.

Oh, I do have one extra addition – pots of *Humea elegans*, the incense plant, raised from seed and enjoyed for their headily aromatic foliage. The seed came from Chatsworth and so always reminds me of the delights of the Palace of the Peaks. Plants with an association are one of gardening's greatest pleasures.

My first ever greenhouse, built from polythene and timber offcuts at the age of 12, measured 3 foot by 6 foot. My first 'proper' greenhouse was bought from Harry Hollings, one of the older men in the parks department nursery where I had my first job. It was made of painted timber and measured 6 foot by 8 foot. My current model is around 18 foot by 10 foot and constructed from powder-coated aluminium alloy, which is virtually maintenance free. We wash it down inside and out once a year in late winter and that is all the maintenance it needs, aside from an occasional drop of oil on the door and on the ventilator hinges.

Instead of painting the glass with a pale green 'whitewash' known as 'Summer Cloud', as I used to do all those years ago (washing it off each autumn to allow maximum light transmission), my present greenhouse is fitted with exterior blinds that can be raised and lowered by pulling on a sprung cord as the rays of the sun dictate. Luxury!

Water is collected from the gutters in a tank, which is sunk into the ground beneath the staging, and transferred to my watering can with a bilge pump. Primitive, but effective.

Ask me in ten years' time what my greenhouse looks like and I will probably describe what you see now. It may be unadventurous, but it keeps me happy (and dry on rainy days). The funny thing is, however sophisticated my later greenhouses, they never eclipse the joy of that first one made from a couple of yards of polythene and a few lumps of wood. Funny that.

The Titchmarsh patent greenhouse mixture – unchanged in fifty years ...

The meadow in high season

It was a labour of love. It must have been, since I sowed it by hand. I had intended to use an old 'seed fiddle' which I had bought at a farm auction. These wonderful implements really do look like something Yehudi Menuhin might have wielded, with a 'bow' that turns a spinning disc which, in turn, broadcasts the seed. But it broke after a few minutes and refused to be repaired. So I got a bucket and scattered the seed over two acres of freshly cultivated ground. (Wild flower seeds will seldom germinate reliably when sown on established pasture, since existing grass offers too much competition.) For just over an hour I traversed the land, to and fro, singing softly, 'We plough the fields and scatter ...'.

I sowed the seed in October, since the repeated freezing and thawing provided by British winters encourages our native wild flowers to germinate better than a spring sowing. Emorsgate's Cricklade Mixture was chosen since it is recommended for chalky downland like mine. But I also invested in a bag of Dame Miriam Rothschild's 'Farmer's Nightmare', which was offered at an eye-watering price in an upmarket gardening magazine.

The germination rate of both types was good, but the Cricklade Mixture has turned out to be far more varied and elegant in its make-up than Dame Miriam's confection, which seems to have a preponderance of clover and cocksfoot grass (*Dactylis glomerata*) and is much more beefy. It tends to collapse in midsummer.

After five years there is still a marked difference between the two areas, and the Cricklade Mixture has won my heart. How could it not? I watch with delight as, following the cowslips of spring, crested dogstail and quaking grass, sterile brome and finer grasses, along with assorted hawkweeds and vetches, umbellifers and scabious, knapweed, marguerites, bird's foot trefoil, clover and mignonette, wild carrot and black medick ... well, the list goes on, and each year offers a slightly different effect, thanks to some species that proliferate in one year and then fizzle out a bit the next.

Rides are mown through the grass – either in sinuous fashion, or to create avenues lined with limes, beech trees or flowering cherries – and maintained every week.

Clare Tupman's steel horse's head (left) is a focal point in a vista that cuts through grasses and wild flowers including wild carrot (right), which changes year on year.

I can't tell you the delight the wild flower meadow brings. Standing on the mound that we made in 2010, I can survey the scene and marvel at the view. In the distance is the spire of the village church – not quite Salisbury Cathedral as painted by Constable, but to me every bit as imposing a focal point.

I planted four mature oak trees in the meadow – each about 15 feet high. My excuse was that I wanted to see how they performed, but there was also a degree of impatience for maturity that saplings could not provide. It is not something that I would do again, or can recommend. While they have survived, and put on a little more leaf every year, they have taken a deal of establishing, and much water in their first couple of years. Perhaps in three or four years' time they will have recovered from the shock. I should have known better …

There are those who say that all topsoil should be scraped off before a meadow is sown, since wild flowers prefer impoverished soil. Ours was rich farmland. I did not intend to go in for land clearance. The result has been tremendously satisfactory, and the introduction of yellow rattle (*Rhinanthus minor*) – a semi-parasite on grass – has reduced the vigour of the sward, which might otherwise compete. It is the only seed that I would recommend for sowing directly onto an established meadow in autumn, since it will germinate in spring and weaken the grass.

We cut the 'hay' in late September or early October (once the seed has fallen) and rake it off. That is the only cultivation the meadow gets and all it appears to need. Year on year our meadow seems to improve, and our tally of wild flowers now stands at ninety-three. It gives me as much pleasure as any part of my garden. 🌱

Bird's foot trefoil, self-heal and white clover thrive on a patch of meadow that is mown once a week until mid-June (left and right) and then left uncut until autumn.

Alan's bees

I visited Alan's garden on a gorgeous summer's day with the sole purpose of counting bees. There were lots to count; in most gardens you can expect to see around six species of bumblebee, but here there were eight. Alongside common species such as the common carder, red-tailed, garden, white-tailed, early and buff-tailed bumblebees were two species of cuckoo bumblebee (which, like their namesake, lay eggs in other bees' nests), as well as honeybees and solitary leafcutters. No wonder there was such a buzz about the garden!

Alan's meadow was sown using a native wild flower mix which includes clover and tufted vetch. The pollen from these plants is particularly good for bumblebees because it is a rich source of protein. This 'superfood' pollen is gathered by the workers and fed to the grubs back in the nest to ensure a healthy next generation of bees. One of the best pollen plants is red clover, which Alan has in plentiful supply.

The garden isn't just popular with bees; butterflies, hoverflies and beetles are also found in abundance. It's wonderful to see such a beautiful garden providing homes for wildlife – especially in a time when some species are struggling to survive. It just goes to show how easily garden habitats can be created, and how fascinating and rewarding they can be.

Kate Bradbury
Wild bee enthusiast

The south terrace

It sounds so delightful and rather grand – like something that might run alongside Lord Emsworth's Blandings Castle. In reality the south-facing terrace is about 85 feet long, of York stone paving, dividing borders alongside the house from borders a foot below it, which are adjacent to the lawn. They are the sunniest borders in the garden and those next to the lawn are home to catmint and alliums, lavender and irises, while those next to the house walls boast tender perennials such as salvias and diascias, as well as *Melianthus major* and the lovely *Lobelia tupa* – a slightly tender perennial with rigid, metre-high stems clad in oval, downy leaves and spires of scarlet summer flowers.

A real corker of a plant, this lobelia was introduced to me by the garden designer Martin Lane Fox, and it was in Martin's Dorset garden that I first saw anything planted in massive pots. Until then, my idea of a 'massive' pot was one more than 14 inches in diameter. I came back from Martin's garden with different ideas, and decided on a row of seven lollipop yew trees in large terracotta pots evenly spaced along the border below the south terrace. Since then I have been convinced of their virtues in giving any garden form and scale – whatever the time of year.

Fewer, larger containers always have more impact than a vast collection of smaller ones, and nowhere is this proved better than with these yews. The containers themselves are Italian Terrace Pots, 'Vaso Archi', 80cm in height and diameter, with a Gothic arch pattern about their rim. They age beautifully, taking on a dusky patina to the terracotta, which is not as vivid an orange as its British counterpart. They have also withstood freezing temperatures in at least two severe winters.

Around the flagstones on which the pots stand I planted 'Hidcote' lavender, which manages to survive for about three years before it needs to be replaced. I clip over

Eryngium Graham Stuart Thomas's selection (left) pushes up year after year with little encouragement and (right) the yew lollipops, box balls and cones make their impact on the south terrace amid catmint and lavender.

the plants after flowering, but the soil in this border is inclined to be damp – perhaps it is the drainage from the terrace – and they rarely survive longer. Bearded irises struggled, too, so as a result I have replaced them with a mixture of pink and white astrantias, which love the sunshine and damp roots (a classic case of finding the right plant to suit the prevailing soil and light conditions).

Catmint doesn't mind it, though, and spills onto the lawn, in spite of my endeavours to restrain it with wire supports, but Spud, our black-and-white cat, loves it and so I turn a blind eye until late June when it is hacked back and manages a second flush before autumn. Along the edge of the terrace, above the pots of yew and planted in holes where paving slabs were omitted, are balls and cones of clipped box. They seem to enjoy the cool root run, though in prolonged dry spells we run the hosepipe into their 'squares' just to make sure they don't become thirsty.

Real spectacle is provided at the eastern end of the terrace. Here there are two raised beds where I have planted *Agapanthus* 'Catharina' – a hardy African lily with flowers carried on stalks 3 feet high.

It is one of those plants that I watch patiently throughout the year. In winter its fleshy, strappy green leaves eventually turn straw-coloured and are pulled off. The bed is bare – time for a helping of well-rotted manure on a mild day. Before long, fresh green leaves emerge, and in June the very first of the flower buds will be visible, like fleshy drumsticks pushing up from the bright green fans of foliage. In late July they open and the beds take on their most spectacular appearance –

awash with sky-blue umbels of flower for several weeks. Never was anticipation better rewarded. Never was the postponement of gratification more amply recompensed. I take friends to see them and try not to look too pleased with myself.

Then the flowers fade and we chop back the stems so that only a sea of waving foliage remains. But next year ... ❦

Agapanthus 'Catharina' fills two raised beds (left and below) alongside the terrace and in late July they open their sky-blue umbels of flower that last for weeks. The meadow (overleaf) surrounding the wildlife pond in high summer.

Dahlias by the caravan

Obsessed since childhood with Kenneth Grahame's
The Wind in the Willows, I bought a gypsy caravan around
25 years ago when the girls were small. I have always
thought the character for whom I feel most empathy in
that wonderful book is Mole – happy on his own for most
of the time, pottering away on (or in) the land – but there
are times when Toad comes to the fore and I have ideas
above my station. Toad buys a caravan (and then a fast
car – but that comes later) and it struck me as a lovely way
of introducing the girls to the great outdoors. Not that we
went anywhere. It was parked at the top of the garden at
Barleywood and we slept in it occasionally overnight, after
I had cooked sausages on the little stove and wrapped
them in slices of bread (as in one of *their* favourite books,
Roald Dahl's *Danny, The Champion of the World*).

Now the girls have grown up, but our first grandchild has
arrived and the caravan awaits its second intake. I have
the storybooks ready.

It sits now in or out of its own shed, depending upon
the weather, and around are planted the golden oat
(*Stipa gigantea*), other grasses and, occasionally, dahlias –
underrated plants for providing late summer colour.
Well, I say 'underrated', but that applies only to those
who refuse to grow them on account of the fact that they
are perceived as vulgar – rather like chrysanthemums.
I love them – especially the cactus types with their spiky
flowers – and I value them, too, for the fact that they are
great for cutting. I shall continue to grow them, and to
keep the caravan in good order for the day when, once
again, I can read: 'The Mole had been working very hard
all the morning ...'

Not the prettiest of names
– *Dahlia* 'Kenora Macop-B'
(below) – but a handsome and
richly coloured cactus-flower
nonetheless.

Choosing plants

At the risk of joining the football pundits, gardening, for me, is a game of two halves: the enjoyment of growing things, and the challenge of positioning plants so they look good individually and yet complement their neighbours – either by contrasting or harmonising. Sometimes a combination works and sometimes it does not, so the challenge is always ongoing.

It was the architect Sir Frederick Gibberd who said that gardening was the most difficult art form of all, since it uses not only colour, texture, scale and form but also time – time in terms of months of the year, and also in the years themselves. As a result, schemes that were once a thing of beauty prove not to be a joy forever, and the gardener must unpick and start again. Unpicking is a thing I seem to do a lot in my garden. Every now and then I will clear a whole border in one go and endeavour to draw up a master plan, but more usually my renovations involve parts of a bed or border, since the scheme may not have gone 'over the hill' in its entirety.

I wonder, sometimes, if I am not as adventurous as I should be, since I use again and again plants that I know to be worthy occupants of the garden. Their worth is judged on several criteria but involves, most importantly, an ability to do well without too much fuss (another way of saying 'the right plant for the right place'). I also demand a reasonably long season of interest (or else a shorter one that has to be supremely spectacular), and an ability to be useful when they are not at their peak of flowering – either as background or infill. The ability to die gracefully is a much-overlooked attribute when it comes to plants.

Having said all that, I am prepared to make exceptions for plants I adore. Delphiniums are so spectacular that I turn a blind eye to their appearance after flowering and the fact that their lower leaves become pale and tatty even before the flowers open (I mask them with foreground geraniums). The agapanthus are glorious for a month, but at least their foliage is smart and green when they have given their all. Geraniums, astrantias, hostas, penstemons, diascias, hemerocallis and sedums are highly revered. Slug damage on hostas apart, they always seem to be giving of their best, and their best suits me fine. ❧

Clockwise from top left: *Penstemon* 'Sour Grapes' – I overwinter cuttings in a cold frame every winter; a self-seeded poppy (I almost always leave them alone); *Geranium* 'Nimbus' alongside the purple-flushed foliage of *Sedum* 'Matrona'; *Hemerocallis* 'Sammy Russell'.

West garden in August

In the part of the garden to the west of the house I've planted classic 'English herbaceous borders'. Although they might seem unadventurous, they are a real challenge to construct. Many are superb from late spring to midsummer, but it is in late summer and autumn that they can be found out. The challenge lies in ensuring a continuity of interest from May right through to October or even November in a mild autumn. Michaelmas daisies

A bumblebee on *Sedum* 'Matrona' (below). Monarda, sedums, anthemis and other border perennials (right) make late summer a billowing delight.

(perennial asters), rudbeckias, heleniums, the later-flowering crocosmias, phlox and sedums are all useful in prolonging the display: there is nothing sadder than an herbaceous border that is 'blown' by late July.

The trouble is that most gardeners visit their local nursery or garden centre in May and June and choose things that are in bud or in flower at the time. If only they would return once a month from then on, then they could ensure their garden had a much longer season of

interest. It was the novelist and gardener H. E. Bates who had a garden which, he said, did not come into its own until September. To see it in all its glory when the gardens of his friends were over the hill gave him great pleasure.

It was also H. E. Bates who coined one of my favourite garden aphorisms: 'Gardening, like love, is a funny thing, and does not always yield to analysis'. It is a saying that continues to provide me with great comfort and solace when my best-laid plans go awry. 🌱

The south terrace through the seasons

The great thing about topiary shapes is that they give the garden year-round structure. I love their lengthening shadows as we pass Midsummer's Day and their ability to retain my garden's form through the winter. In spring (top right) the border below the yew lollipops is peppered with *Allium* 'Purple Sensation'. In summer (main picture) the agapanthus rivet all eyes, and by October (centre right) the borders are beginning to turn russet as the leaves of shrubs and perennials take on whatever autumn tints they offer. I sigh at the arrival of this 'season of straw', but the birds love it. In winter snowfall (bottom right) the garden has a crackling silence and the topiary is transformed (until I knock off the snow to avoid broken branches!).

Autumn

Autumn is a
turning point;
the moment at
which control of
my garden seems
to slip though my
fingers ...

Introduction

It seems to me that you can smell autumn before you can see it. There will be a morning in my garden – in September or, in some years, early October – when there is in the air that faint acrid tang which is a dead give-away that the growing season is coming to a close. It is a sweet-and-sour confection of aromas that hints at decay. It happens every year and fills me with a sense of wistfulness; knowing that what did not come right this year will now have to wait until next.

It is not always a sad moment, but it is invariably one of resignation, and I console myself that without autumn there would be no spring. It is another of those reminders of the pleasures of gardening in a cool, temperate climate rather than the tropics – the prospect of no discernible difference between the seasons fills me with dread.

The pattern, though, has undoubtedly changed since my childhood. Seed packets bought from Woolworths suggested, in the 1950s, that parsnips should be sown in February. Nowadays we'll be lucky to get on to the soil much before April. Dahlias would be frosted and blackened in September; now they can last until October or November. The seasons have shifted – spring can come later and summer (or what passes for it) can run on longer before the weather turns chilly.

Do we need to worry? Well, we need to be considerate in our care for the environment, that's for certain, to avoid blasting it with chemicals at every possible opportunity; to refrain from being control freaks and from expecting Nature to be consistent and benign when she is, historically, anything but.

And yet, like many gardeners who have endured as many wet summers as droughts and as mild winters as bitter ones, I am rather more sanguine about the changing nature of the seasons than many whose opinions on 'climate change' and 'global warming' tend to verge on the hysterical. Of course, to admit as much is to be branded a 'climate change denier', which is both unfair and inaccurate. I'd be better disposed towards those who foretell the worst if they told the whole story, not just selected highlights that serve their own opinions.

The winter garden border dwindling into autumn – the purple and gold of summer is added to by russets and oranges as the nights turn colder …

I have never heard mention of the warm tropical periods between the dozen Ice Ages the Earth has endured over the last million years. Climate naturally changes; what we must not do is exacerbate it. It is undeniable that the activities of man can adversely affect the environment, but then so can Nature; it's a bit misleading – and typically self-centred – to lay the blame entirely at our door. But this is a book about my garden; not a tirade against those whose opinions are designed to depress … as autumn could if we were not careful.

There are bright colours of leaf to admire, and berries, and those strange flowers which, in spite of having had a spring and summer to get their act together, prefer to reserve their colourful display until autumn. They may be eccentric in that regard, but as a result they are all the more welcome.

Of course, for a gardener like me who enjoys order, if not strict formality, autumn can be a time of anxiety. There are leaves on the lawn. Winds can damage branches. Heavy rains can lay low my Michaelmas daisies. But I calm myself in the knowledge that the cleansing operation has begun; that I am being given a chance to accomplish even better things next year. Nature's dustpan and brush is sweeping aside a year of 'not so goods' and 'might have beens' in order that I be given another chance to do even better in a few months' time.

And that's what autumn is, really, a second chance. I must approach it after the fashion of Winston Churchill and regard it not so much as the 'beginning of the end', but the 'end of the beginning'. That way, climate change or no, I have a chance of holding on to at least a modicum of optimism. 🌱

Hostas in pots (left) begin to show their buttery autumn tints from September, and the seedheads of agapanthus will soon turn strawy white. As the weather gets colder (right) the heavily laden cockspur thorn (*Crataegus crus-galli*) is slowly stripped by blackbirds who come at it from all directions.

The south garden

Autumn comes early to some plants. The deeply veined leaves of the Persian ironwood (*Parrotia persica*), for instance, begin to take on reddish tints in August. Other plants start in midsummer and run on into autumn. I love *Hydrangea arborescens* 'Annabelle' for her outrageously showy mop-heads which start to form in June in a shade of lime green, gradually expanding into plump white clouds which simply smother the shrub from late July and on into autumn. In winter they turn papery. It is a prolonged season of interest for which I am grateful – grateful enough to have planted eight specimens in the borders around the dolphin pond. They increase in size year on year, and the largest – and oldest at five years – is now 5 feet high and 6 feet across.

Annabelle's only disadvantage is that she does not have stems of a strength and rigidity commensurate with her floral generosity. Most plants that are 'floppers' I cope with for a few years and then replace with more sturdy, self-supporting varieties, but for Annabelle I make an exception. The faded flowerheads are cut back in early spring to two strong buds. When planting new bushes in late winter I slip circular wire supports of the type used for peonies over the stems, whose leaves then grow to mask them. I never remove these supports and they stay in place year on year. Annabelle has her corset and I am happy to keep her secret – because she's worth it. 🌿

The south garden in early autumn, with 'Annabelle' doing her bit around the dolphin pond, beyond the soft purple 'gauze' of *Verbena bonariensis*.

The grass border

Around the back of the barn we built a brick-and-flint retaining wall to hold back what had previously been an unrestrained bank of earth. On the pillars that supported it I positioned terracotta 'Swag and Acanthus' pots from Jim Keeling's Whichford Pottery, planting them up with clipped box balls to make living finials. But I also wanted a narrow border atop the wall – just a foot and a half wide – to act as a junction between the cultivated garden and the wild flower meadow beyond. Grasses seemed the obvious answer and I planted a mixture of them to create a long and feathery ribbon that allows the garden to fray into the landscape. In late summer and autumn this grassy ribbon comes into its own when the feathery plumes turn to light-catching silver and gold.

I can't claim much credit for anything other than the planting, since the grasses really do look after themselves and the weak and feeble ones have been forced out over the years by those of a stronger constitution. This suits me fine.

So happy are these grasses in the well-drained earth above the wall that some of them run into the lawn alongside. Only regular mowing prevents them from travelling further, so if you want to avoid really invasive species, steer clear of the grey-leafed *Leymus arenarius* and gardener's garters – *Phalaris arundinacea* var. *picta* – both of which are excessively rampant and only recommended where they can have as much ground as they like. Under these circumstances you will be happy to praise them for their accommodating nature.

With grasses, it is the ability of their delicate and feathery foliage and flowerheads to contrast with the solid nature of stone, brick and terracotta that I find appealing, and within mixed beds and borders they make a wonderful 'glue' that allows plants which would otherwise sit uncomfortably alongside one another to co-exist in a much more pleasing way. Grasses, if you like, are the peacemakers of the border. 🌱

Chinese silver grass (*Miscanthus sinensis*) contrasts with terracotta pots and spheres of box, and frames the statue of Peter Pan on an autumn day.

The meadow and the wildlife pond

The meadow is at its most spectacular between April and
August, when a succession of flowers – from cowslips
at the start of the season, to knapweed and scabious as
the summer days stretch out – are giving their all. By
September the grass has turned to hay and the moment
comes for the annual harvest. It is a daunting time –
the grass and wild flowers must be cut and removed –
preferably with all speed, since to leave the cut grass lying

The hay is cut in the wild flower
meadow (below) and for a couple
of weeks it is only the rides that
are green and pleasant. The
residents of the duck house
(right) have moved on, and now
it serves as garden sculpture
and a reminder of ill-advised
MPs ...

on the surface for more than a couple of days will result in the underlying sward being burnt by the heat of the remains decomposing on top. And so we wait and watch the weather forecast until assured of several days of dry weather. And then we cut, and rake, and cart away, and the only sign of green on the meadow is the mown rides that have been cut among the flowers.

Having tried assorted methods of cutting, we now do the job with a small John Deere tractor mower, which has the ability to cut long grass and throw it up into a small covered trailer that is towed behind. When this trailer is full we dump the hay in one spot and then manhandle it onto the trailer of the Land Rover before carting it away.

The timing of the operation is critical, since we want the seeds from the majority of the wild flowers to have formed and fallen before the hay is removed. Do the job too early and the seed has not ripened; too late and the risk of prolonged bad weather makes cutting difficult. There is relief when the job is done, even though the shorn meadow looks a little bald for a few weeks. Several days of showery weather is all it takes to bring about the haze of green that will yield next year's flowers, and a guessing game as to which species will predominate, since the precise nature of the mixture varies year on year.

The wildlife pond, too, is winding down after a year of fecundity: the dragonflies and damselflies cease to be active, though the roach will still come to the surface of the water in a feeding frenzy when thrown some food; only declining to eat when the weather turns cold when they prefer to skulk in the depths. The heron has a tougher job finding lunch now.

The duck house has given rise to teasing, since one ill-advised Member of Parliament attempted to pass the cost of his as an expense. But Ivor Ingall, the designer and maker of the 'Stockholm' duck house that graces our pond, is a neighbour whose handiwork I am proud to display. The structure is hugely successful for us. In summer 2012 it brought off two broods of mallards – one of 12 and another of 14 – and when vacated by the ducklings it was taken over by moorhens. In their interests I shall continue to suffer the slings and arrows ...

Berries in the meadow

The native hedgerow that we planted around the meadow is a rewarding mixture of hawthorn and field maple, holly and sweet briar, dog rose and dogwood. It acts as a wildlife corridor – a home to shrews and voles, field mice and weasels, and is a haven for nesting birds. In spring the hawthorn makes a creamy waterfall; in early summer the hedge is studded with single pink roses courtesy of the briars, and in autumn there are bright red berries glinting in the gloom. I trim it a little in late winter – once the berries have all been plundered and before there is a danger of birds prospecting for nesting sites – and it is thickening up nicely after five years.

There is something hugely satisfying about gardening for wildlife; a vindication, if you like, of being a gardener. I still feel a thrill when a robin or a blackbird perches on a tree I have planted, when nest-boxes are colonized by a chattering of blue tits, and when bird feeders filled with nyjer seed are patronised by a charm of goldfinches.

But aside from birds and 'cuddly' mammals, I am eager to encourage the 'ugly sisters' of the natural world – the beetles and the earthworms, the centipedes and the ladybirds, the spiders and insects that are every bit as important in the cycle of Nature.

Butterflies, in particular, are a delight, and we plant not only the nectar-rich sedums and buddleias from which the adults drink their fill, but also food plants for the caterpillars. A clump of nettles in a sunny spot is often recommended as a nursery for small tortoiseshells and red admirals, peacocks and painted ladies, yet all too often it becomes nothing more than a clump of nettles in a sunny spot and a stinging sensation on summer-naked limbs.

But patience can be rewarded, and there are other plants to cherish – thistles and meadow grasses, common and alder buckthorn which will feed the larvae of the bravest of butterflies, the brimstone, which flits around my garden in March.

The list of butterflies spotted in the meadow continues to grow; all the expected kinds are there – from meadow browns and skippers to the gatekeeper, the ringlet and the blues – but the appearance of the green hairstreak last summer gave me the greatest pleasure. Its food plant is the bird's foot trefoil (*Lotus corniculatus*), which is present in abundance in the meadow. To know that the butterfly found it and hopefully raised another brood makes meadow gardening all the more worthwhile. ❦

Clockwise from top: the juicy, translucent berries of the guelder rose (*Viburnum opulus*); the rusty pear is enveloped in fading wild flowers; rose hips in the meadow hedge; the black berries of the common buckthorn (*Rhamnus cathartica*) whose leaves are a food plant for the brimstone butterfly.

The west garden and the terrace

The corner at the 'sharp end' of the terrace points due south and so sees sun for most of the day, even if its rays do have to shine through an assortment of trees to make their presence felt. Glinting between the chestnut and the yew and the ash, they reach this spot for much of the day and it is the perfect place for meals when I have been chained to my desk all morning.

By late summer the borders here are beginning to be overblown, with many of the earlier-flowering plants running to seed, but deadheading is one of my favourite jobs, and most plants will be happy to put out a second, albeit smaller, flush of flowers if the earlier lot are snipped away after they fade and before seed is set.

I am not one for excessive staking – trussed-up perennials that look like oven-ready Christmas turkeys are not my idea of a thing of beauty – so some plants do tend to flop a bit. Deadheading, though, appeals to my sense of order, as well as being a way of prolonging the interest of a bed or border. With a wicker basket over my arm and a small pair of secateurs in my hand I can be happily occupied for an hour or more, confident that when I finish a particular bed or border it will look refreshed and revitalised.

Sedums and the blue spires of perovskia provide the flower power, and the seedheads of globe artichoke and one or two other perennials are enjoyed by the birds on the border beside the terrace.

Flowers which give rise to decorative seedheads are left for our amusement and as food for the birds, and I try my best to keep the garden going by planting later blooms – phlox and rudbeckias, heleniums and the later crocosmias – that will see us on into autumn. I couldn't help but feel a little let down by Vita Sackville-West's admission that the garden at Sissinghurst was overblown and finished by August, but then those were the days – during the first half of the twentieth century – when the aristocracy took off to foreign climes or the grouse moor at the end of summer and it mattered not that their garden's glory was spent. Barring the odd fortnight, we tend to stick around longer and I like my plants to do the same.

Weeds – the bane of any gardener's life – are not much of a problem; certainly not in autumn. It stands to reason that if you clear the ground of any thick-rooted perennial weeds at the outset, enrich the soil with well-rotted compost or manure and plant beds and borders relatively thickly, by the summer of the first season after planting there will be simply no room for 'new' weeds to grow – apart from the odd one or two which can be pulled up by hand as soon as they are spotted. Among shrubs, which need wider spacing and therefore are surrounded by bare soil for longer than more closely spaced and faster-growing border perennials, a 2-inch-thick chipped bark mulch will suppress any errant weed growth and prevent moisture evaporation. By the time the bark has rotted away – in two or three years' time – the foliage covers the ground. It sounds simple, but that's because it is.

It is not until late summer that the lollipops of yew are given their annual clip. Oh, there are those who suggest that topiary yew and hedges should be trimmed twice a year, but somehow we never get round to it. I rather like their woolly appearance in July and August and the chance to trim them (always with hand shears, never with powered trimmers) gives a sense of freshness and renewal at a time of year when the prevailing feeling is one of tiredness and winding down. Clipped closely in September or October, their growth spurt is all but finished and they will stay trim and crisp of shape until late the following spring.

The box is ideally trimmed in June, but we have so much of it that the job tends to drag on into July and August, with the odd snip here and there in September if growth has been excessive. The 'spats' round the avenue of *Pyrus calleryana* 'Chanticleer' are usually given two haircuts a year – in June and again in September, if the season has been moist enough to encourage excessive growth.
I never tire of looking down this vista, which terminates in an urn at one end and a glazed French pot containing a topiary chicken at the other. Simple pleasures …

Spud at fifteen (left) – at home with a lollipop. The avenue of *Pyrus calleryana* 'Chanticleer' (below), each surrounded by a 'spat' of clipped box.

With the shortening days comes the burnishing of foliage; gently at first, amounting to no more than a hint of bronzing. It happens on all kinds of plants; the leaves become more leathery and weatherbeaten before they fall. Not all plants produce what can properly be called 'autumn colour', but most undergo some kind of chemical change which alters their texture and to some degree their appearance.

Spiders are more in evidence now, stringing their webs where they are most inconvenient – across pathways, and often well below head height. On chilly mornings their gossamer is beaded with dew and it is impossible not to be impressed at their weaving abilities and intimate knowledge of civil engineering. Where they are especially elaborate I make a detour – it seems heartless to destroy the fruits of their labours with a single sweep of the hand or the hoe. Perhaps I'm just too soft …

The one thing I resent more than any other in autumn is the move back into wellies. After a summer of light shoes (I can never bring myself to wear sandals) I must climb back into the old rubber boots for my early morning walk around the garden. The dew is heavier now, and just as eighteenth- and nineteenth-century sailors seldom learned to swim (it being considered bad luck to do so), this twenty-first-century gardener has an aversion to wet feet. The profound agony of cold, damp socks in flimsy shoes is not something to which I will ever become accustomed. My desert island luxury? A pair of neoprene-lined wellington boots. 'Season of mists and' … dry feet.

A garden spider (left) spins an autumn web; an autumn mixture (right) of the wedding cake tree (*Cornus controversa* 'Variegata'), cut-leaved purple elder (*Sambucus nigra* 'Black Lace'), a clipped bay tree, blue-flowered campanula and *Artemisia* 'Powis Castle'.

Humphry Repton
never says much,
in spite of the
fact that I always
wish him 'good
morning' ...

The drive

I have a friend whose garden is full of evergreens, simply because she hates the untidiness of fallen leaves. There are times when I sympathise, but even evergreens shed their leaves – usually in June when they are least welcome and you want the garden to look its pristine best.

The waves of box on the drive are heavily spattered with fallen leaves from the trees above in autumn, but the effect is not necessarily unpleasant – just a reminder of the season. The snowy mespilus (*Amelanchier lamarckii*) takes on wonderful fiery tints and its fallen leaves are small enough to fall down through the box and be lost from view. Not so those of the ash and maple, which sit like litter atop the rolling main. They are scooped off every week or so.

It's tempting, with fallen leaves, to let them lie until the entire tree is bare, then undertake one mammoth clear-up operation. But if fallen leaves form a thick carpet on the lawn for several weeks, there is a real danger that the grass will be killed. The same is true on herbaceous borders, and so the painstaking job of clearing them and composting them on a weekly basis begins. We put ours in a large post-and-wire bin and rot them down over a year or two; there is no rush. In smaller gardens they can be put, while moist, into black bin liners that have been perforated with a fork. They may take a year or two to rot down even here, but the resulting leafmould is a valuable soil conditioner.

The drive is not long, but because it curves it reveals the garden gradually – first the waves of box and the trees above them, in leaf or berry, followed by the arc of conical yew trees which frame the transparent sphere of water and then Peter Pan at the top of the slope. After ten years I still enjoy this changing view as I walk or drive up to the house, looking to see if something could be better placed or improved upon. 🌱

Looking down the drive (left) the berries of the cockspur thorn (*Crataegus crus-galli*) drip from its branches in autumn. A terracotta jar (below) sits among the waves of box.

The chestnut border

After its spring show of snowdrops and dwarf narcissi, dog's tooth violets and hellebores, the chestnut border slips into a period of torpor, thanks to the dense canopy of leaves above. *Tellima grandiflora* and *Brunnera macrophylla* tolerate the deep shade and do their bit, along with Turk's cap lilies and the redoubtable *Campanula poscharskyana*, which tumbles over the low retaining wall where the light is brighter. But only the yellow-variegated *Euonymus* 'Emerald 'n' Gold' and the cream-variegated *Euonymus* 'Emerald Gaiety' really sing out from the gloom. These two evergreen plants really do deserve a place in any garden. They are seldom singled out for praise, but are so deliciously undemanding and versatile, as well as being good-looking all year round. They grow readily, but not problematically so, into low scone-like domes, and can be clipped into formal topiary shapes or left to their own devices. Put them against a wall and they will climb. The only care and attention they demand is that any plain green shoots that arise are snipped out so that they do not take over. Proper little earners they are, and I am grateful for them under the conker tree where they have the stage almost to themselves in summer.

It's not really a disadvantage, since other parts of the garden rivet the eye from May to September and little is expected of this over-canopied bed, but when the chestnut leaves begin to fall, more light enters, and the autumn-flowering *Cyclamen hederifolium* pushes up its pale pink flowers as a reminder of the changing seasons. It can only be in my imagination that it seems to flower earlier each year; 'why does summer go so quickly … ?' Up come those delicate reflex-petalled flowers among a carpet of ivy and assorted ground-hugging foliage, and they give us pastel colour for several weeks before the stalks turn into watch-springs and plunge their seeds down into the ground. It's a neat and effective trick, and a top-dressing of chipped bark or leafmould makes sure the seeds have a suitable environment in which to germinate and increase the colony.

The sun is lower now, flooding the front of the mellow brick house with amber light when it rises above the tall Leyland hedge in the early afternoon. From now on the garden's topiary comes into its own. When deciduous plants are beginning to lose their form, along with their foliage, the evergreens turn into the equivalent of gnomons on sundials – reflecting the time of day in the angle and the ever-increasing length of their shadows. It is another reason to be wistful, another reminder that winter is not far away … 🌱

The dainty flowers of *Cyclamen hederifolium* (left) push up from the scattering of fallen leaves in September and October.

Variegated euonymus (right) shines under the chestnut tree, and the afternoon sun bathes the house in an amber glow.

Cherry trees in autumn

If their flowering season is brief each spring, their autumn glory is even shorter lived, but flowering cherries really do give their all in their two seasons of spectacle.

My first memory of flowering cherries is of the variety oft planted as a street tree in the 1950s – 'Kanzan' – whose open shuttlecock shape and profusion of coconut-ice-pink flowers have made it the bane of every plant snob. True, it is not the most graceful of trees, neither is it possessed of any subtlety when in flower, but to drive down a street of 'Kanzan' in full flower and not be capable of saying 'wow' is to admit to an overriding degree of cynicism. Subtle? No. Spectacular? Definitely, even if the spectacle has more than a touch of Disney World about it.

Other flowering cherries get a better press, and my own favourite is 'Shirotae'. I have planted an avenue of this variety, whose double flowers are pink in the bud, fading eventually to white and carried on a tree of more arching grace than the much-maligned 'Kanzan'. The unfurling leaves of 'Shirotae' are tinged with bronze-pink, which I find marginally less attractive then the varieties whose leaves are fresh green and leave the colour spectacle to the blossom alone. Other folk prefer the full Monty – bright pink blossom and purple leaves. This, I confess, is a tinge too far even for me.

In autumn most cherries offer spectacular foliage tints that few would complain about, and if winds are light and temperatures lower gradually they can be admirable for two or three weeks. Rapidly dropping temperatures and high winds will shorten the spectacle, but the sight of them is still astonishing, especially against a clear blue sky.

My own trees, growing on soil overlying chalk, suffer few problems, apart from occasional outbreaks of cherry blackfly in late spring and early summer, which causes the growing shoot tips to become puckered and distorted. Affected leaves turn brown and fall. In a wet summer they gradually recover from this deformity. For organic gardeners like me, 'winter washes' that kill the overwintering aphid eggs are not an option, but watering young trees well in dry summers should help them get over the attacks, and mild soapy water can be sprayed on to reduce the severity of the infestation.

In late spring 2012 wood pigeons were a real problem – perching on the branches and tearing at the leaves on all but the ends of the twigs (where they were too fat to be supported). Only the rains allowed the trees to produce more leaves into June and July. I resisted the temptation to make a pigeon pie. Next time I might not …

Prunus 'Shirotae' remains a favourite flowering cherry; its astonishingly bright autumn colour adds to its desirability.

The south terrace

I 'walk the estate' at least once a day. It's a phrase I use ironically, since four acres, while being vast compared with the usual back garden, hardly puts me in the class of landed gentry. But it is easier than saying, 'I'm going round the garden and then round the wild flower meadow at the back of the barn'. There are parts of 'the estate' that engage me more than others, depending on the time of year, but in the garden itself the south terrace almost always has something worth looking at – whether it is topiary in winter or tender flowers in summer.

The great thing about shelter and a sunny aspect is that it prolongs the life of a bed or border, provided the plants do not burn out, and the border at the foot of the south-facing house wall does ring the changes. In summer it erupts with those brightly flowered, tender, shrubby salvias like 'Hot Lips' and 'Mr Bumble', along with diascias and penstemons. The great thing about these three is that they go on and on and on until the frosts, and the penstemons are great for cutting.

But the autumn *pièces de résistance* are the clumps of *Nerine bowdenii* at the very front of the border. They were further back originally – being 45cm tall – but that meant their bulbs were shaded by the foliage of other plants and failed to receive the sun baking they enjoy. So they

A view along the south terrace, brightened by nerines whose starry pink flowers burst open in September and October.

were moved (not something they generally relish) and I got away with it. Now their snake-like stems stretch ever upwards in September and they open their spidery starburst flowers of vibrant pink in that month and the next.

The great thing about these plants is that they thrive on neglect – given that sun-baked spot, where their bulbs are only just below the surface of the soil, they flower generously year after year, the clump continually increasing in size. The green strappy leaves follow the flowers but are not so large that they get in the way of other plants.

The terrace itself is bordered by the lollipop yews in pots, and the lateral axis it forms ends in a seat placed in a rusted iron arbour in the garden at one end and a cluster of artefacts on the wall of the barn at the other – a plaster plaque and the terracotta head of a man flanked by two spiral-clipped box bushes in pots. I like them here, but I'm never sure about spiral-clipped conifers in general – they verge on the fussy – some would say naff.

It is difficult to over-emphasise the importance of focal points. Not only do they draw the eye and point up the geometry of a garden, but they are strangely satisfying to contemplate. I'll often walk to a chosen spot and look in a particular direction, simply for the pleasure of seeing how something lines up. There will be a medical name for it. I probably need to seek attention. But I find such prospects pleasing and very calming. Snipping out a branch here and there, the better to frame a view or reveal a garden ornament, is something that can be achieved in seconds but which will give lasting pleasure. But then I'm a simple soul.

And yet some folk don't seem to see such things. I've been around a number of 'posh' and highly thought-of gardens where really simple things (to my eye) have been overlooked. It's not that I consider myself a great designer (far from it) but spatial awareness and an eye for line, form, scale and perspective do give me pleasure.

Where does an eye for design come from? Is it something we are born with – or without? I think it can be awakened, and looking at gardens designed by those who have it or had it in abundance will help you get your eye in. For me, the work of Arabella Lennox-Boyd, Martin Lane Fox, David Hicks, Tom Stuart-Smith, Robert Myers, Arne Maynard and Luciano Giubbilei will always lift my spirits and, hopefully, my game. 🌱

Clockwise from top left: the sunny border is occupied by plants that appreciate the warmth and shelter of a south-facing house wall: *Salvia uliginosa*; *Hedychium densiflorum* 'Assam Orange'; nerine buds about to burst open; *Diascia personata*.

The greenhouse borders

For years I struggled with the greenhouse borders. They were a delight in spring when planted up with tulips – a different colour scheme each year – but with summer came a challenge. Dahlias grew too large. Cosmos were too floppy. Impatiens fell prey to downy mildew. It was time for a change. I planted a mixture of sun roses (cistus), lavender of the variety 'Imperial Gem' (deeper purple than 'Hidcote' but equally self-supporting) and lady's mantle (*Alchemilla mollis*). Bingo! From early June until the end of the year I have a scheme that seems to look after itself, and there is room to sneak the tulips between them in autumn and tweak them out as their flowers fade. The combination of the three plants I can wholeheartedly recommend for a sunny, well-drained bed or border.

Framing the sphere of water are four quince trees which are studded with lovely large, white 'apple blossom' in spring, but their real season of interest is autumn, when they are simply laden with aromatic fruits that most folk mistake for pears. The variety is 'Meech's Prolific' and it lives up to its promise. Though described as being a touch tender for northern gardens, where it is recommended as being best trained on a sunny wall, in my Hampshire garden it has batted not an eyelid in the last two severe winters.

It is a variety that was discovered by Rev. William Meech in Connecticut in the mid-nineteenth century (which might account for its reputed tenderness) and each fruit can weigh up to half a kilogram. We make them into quince jelly and a heap of them sit in a fruit bowl on the kitchen table in October until they start to turn rotten and the sweet aroma is no more.

Over the last few years the trees have become more shapely, since I go over them a couple of times during the summer (they put on at least a couple of feet a season) snipping back the unwanted young stems which are soft and covered in white down. For several years I laboriously hauled out a stepladder to do this job, until I discovered a pair of 4-foot-long secateurs made by the Dutch firm of De Wiltfang. Not only do they allow me to prune the trees from ground level, they also hold on to the snipped stem so that it can be dropped straight into my prunings basket. For a gardener who verges on the OCD, this is doubly rewarding. 🌱

The quince *Cydonia* 'Meech's Prolific' is heavily laden each autumn and the fruits make tasty quince jelly.

Autumn colour

It took me ages to stop being too tidy. Well, I was trained in a parks department where everything that wasn't attached was swept up, and anything brown was snipped off. Autumn continues to be a challenge to my tidy-mindedness. But it is worth conquering and, in all fairness, its fleeting glories don't last long. It is the garden's last hurrah, and one worth luxuriating in, even though it can be testing.

No garden can match the autumn spectacle of Westonbirt Arboretum or Sheffield Park, but every garden should have a few trees or shrubs that can celebrate what can be the dreariest and dampest of seasons. Japanese maples are among the best plants of diminutive stature to bring autumn colour to small gardens. Last year I planted half a dozen different ones in the border at the back of the garden. They can be a tricky race to establish – some of them more temperamental than others – but among the most reliable, I've found, is *Acer palmatum* 'Elegans' which makes a tree about 8 foot tall in ten years, with widely fingered green leaves that turn orange and yellow before they fall in autumn. Unlike some Japanese maples, it has a real grace. For deep purple leaves, 'Bloodgood' takes some beating, and while I like 'Sango-kaku' (which

Betula utilis var. *jacquemontii* towers over Miss Willmott's ghost – *Eryngium giganteum* – which seeds itself about the border below, coming a close second to Solomon's seal (*Polygonatum multiflorum*) which spreads by underground rhizomes. Both offer colourful autumn interest.

used to be called 'Senkaki') for its pink young stems and orange-yellow autumn colour, with me, it has a tendency to lose a few stems each year to die-back. Still, all Japanese maples are worth experimenting with.

Birches are good trees for small gardens. They may grow quite tall, but their canopy remains feathery and cuts out little of the light that is needed by plants to grow beneath them. My former favourite, *Betula utilis* var. *jacquemontii* has been usurped by *Betula albosinensis* 'Fascination', an upright grower whose young stems are a foxy red while the bark is creamy white with a hint of pink. In autumn the leaves of birches turn bright yellow before falling, peppering the lawn with their fallen foliage which is so light that it seldom causes a problem even for tardy sweeper-uppers.

Of all the semi-mature trees I have planted (and, to be honest, there are not that many, since I prefer vigorous youngsters which will settle in rapidly to older brutes that can sulk) the tulip tree (*Liriodendron tulipifera*) has been the one which established most readily and romped away. I love the shape of the leaves on this tree – tulip like, even though it is the yellow cup-shaped flowers that appear on mature specimens that gave the tree its common name. So vigorous is it that I snip off one or two of the lowest stems each year to allow the plants in the border below it some light, but I don't mind that since it gives real meat to one corner of the garden without being oppressive, and its leaves turn butter-yellow before they fall.

Within the borders autumn colour is equally important, and while it might not encompass the scarlets and crimsons offered by trees, there is still a range of ochres, raw siennas and burnt umbers that make a change from the spring and summer greens.

Grasses are good here, along with plants that produce seedheads that the birds will enjoy – eryngiums, rudbeckias, monardas and the like. Insects, too, enjoy the cover that fading flowers provide, and that's a valid reason which encourages me to stay my hand with the secateurs. I leave these plants for as long as I can bear, but then, when they have all but turned to mush, I snip them off and consign them to the compost heap. Heigh-ho, another year gone …

Autumn colour (left) from *Acer palmatum* 'Elegans'. The tulip tree, (right) *Liriodendron tulipifera*, along with acers and *Molinia caerulea* subsp. *arundinacea* 'Transparent' – the tidiest of ornamental grasses whose stems snap off neatly at the base when they fade.

The dolphin pond

Ponds are generally not much to write home about in autumn, and they do need clearing of fallen leaves if they are not to turn stagnant. That's an easy job with the dolphin pond, given a fishing net and a long arm. We did have a few goldfish in it at first, but even with its raised sides the heron managed to fish it clean within a matter of weeks. Well, not exactly clean, but the fish that

The glory of the garden (below) around the dolphin pond begins to fade but the evergreens come into their own in the form of kerbs and cones of box and lollipops of Portugal laurel. Miss Willmott's ghost – *Eryngium giganteum* (right) – will shed its seeds to provide next year's steely show.

remained skulked at the bottom underneath the fountain to stay out of the way of his spear-like beak. Not exactly ornamental. In the end we gave up on the remaining half dozen, fished them out ourselves and transferred them to the wildlife pond where they co-habit happily with several hundred roach. Even the pygmy waterlilies are only moderately happy here, thanks to the trickle of water from the dolphin's mouth which disturbs a surface that they would prefer to be still, but they do provide at least a little leaf cover on the surface until autumn comes and they die down for another year.

At this time of year the rim of clipped box around the pond provides vital greening up, as does the low box hedge that runs around the edge of the borders. The fountain is turned off in winter, not simply to avoid it freezing, but because if it is left on in damp weather it seems to exacerbate the incidence of box blight on the side where it splashes the bushes. Any precaution that prevents this vile disease from attacking is worth undertaking, and an absence of water splash in winter does seem to help.

The box provides greenery at ground level, but higher up are lollipops of Portugal laurel *(Prunus lusitanica)*. In my parks department days I found this an exceedingly boring shrub, spreading its mantle of Hammer-Horror darkness through countless Victorian shrubberies. But now I value it tremendously as a topiary specimen, whether clipped into orbs, pyramids or cones. It is the most unfussy of shrubs, it withstands all weathers and readily withstands clipping (even butchery when it has outgrown its station). Its leaves might be dark green but they reflect the light on the dullest day. The leaf stalks, should you care to examine them, are tinged with deep crimson, and

white flowers that are carried in long tassels like a hebe decorate the bushes in a good summer.

While the evergreens come to the fore, other plants fade. The white flowerheads of *Hydrangea arborescens* 'Annabelle' are turning brown now. For a few weeks they will look miserable, but then they will turn crisp and I'm happy to leave them on the bushes until early spring when they are clipped off to reveal the new buds below.

The west garden

One thing that the changing seasons do is help you to see your garden differently. They alter your perspective, most obviously by virtue of the falling leaves which reveal views that were not there before. It's one of the reasons why gardening in Britain is so much more refreshing than gardening in the tropics, or even in the Mediterranean. Unchanging views foster a lack of interest and a reduction in our powers of observation. Such is seldom the case on these shores. At least, this is what I tell myself on those dank days when the sky is the colour of an army blanket and everything seems to be dark and drear. Now the wellies are everyday wear, and soggy fallen leaves that refuse to be dislodge themselves on the doormat litter the carpet and give rise to gentle complaint.

But early autumn has its compensations; it is a great time to plant things. The soil is still relatively warm from summer and there is little danger of anything committed to the earth at this time of year drying out. Roots will be established before the bitter winter weather really kicks in. In this respect autumn can be a time of renewal and of birth. At least, that's what I convince myself on those mornings when I look out of the window on to a scene that owes less to 'mists and mellow fruitfulness' than to darkness and decay. It's all for the best, really.

Vertical lines seem to become more evident in autumn – here the trunks of birch trees and *Pyrus calleryana* 'Chanticleer' – and the foliage begins to fade, but there is still colour from crimson-tinted sedums and the grey wiry stems of *Perovskia* 'Blue Spire'.

As the leaves fall and autumn colour becomes just a memory to be swept up and composted, the bark of birches and dogwoods, willows and maples begins to catch the eye, and berries are newly formed on things that you had forgotten about – viburnums and euonymus, roses and hawthorn, buckthorn and privet. You might have forgotten about these bountiful plants, but the birds will not have, and will be waiting.

We feed our birds all the year round, but we ration them in summer since 18-inch-long feeders can be emptied in a day and I want the caterpillars and the greenfly cleared up as well. But from now on the garden is dotted with a few more. Some contain mixed seeds, others peanuts, and there is one for the goldfinches filled with nyjer seeds – those little black seeds that they love every bit as much as the thistle seedheads in the meadow.

It's wonderful how the importation of this seed from Ethiopia (*Guizotia abyssinica*) has encouraged goldfinches into our gardens and presumably increased their numbers. Its only disadvantage is that other birds peck at the grass below the feeder to mop up the spillage, and the result is sour earth and a bare patch on the lawn. Site the feeder over paving and the problem is avoided and the mess can be swept up.

The bones of the garden are showing now, as the flesh falls away, and it's a good time to take stock and see where the structure falls apart. The topiary is more obvious, as are trees that are planted in formal lines and avenues. Areas of little interest become more evident, and the combination of planting opportunity and suitable weather for their establishment makes this a time when I sit down and look through books and catalogues for inspiration. As the garden matures and fills up there is less and less room for newcomers, but this situation has the effect of making me more demanding – biting the bullet and heaving out plants that do not earn their keep and replacing them with something else I want to try; something that will offer better value. Yes; strange as it seems, autumn – the time of year when everything seems to be winding down and falling away – really can be a time of renewal.

Statues become more dominant as the foliage disappears, and they take on even greater importance as focal points – Jim Keeling's statue of Humphry Repton, a stone lion and Nic Fiddian Green's horse's head are even easier to admire when there are fewer distractions.

Pear avenue through the seasons

In autumn (main picture) the low level of the sun can provide unexpected delights on clear days, when the colours of fading leaves are captured and illuminated. But there is no time of year when I do not enjoy the avenue of *Pyrus calleryana* 'Chanticleer'. Sometimes thought of as little more than a useful street tree, it has many advantages in small gardens. It is pyramidal in habit and so does not cut out too much light, produces good autumn colour, blossom in spring (top right), bright green leaves in summer (centre right) and a shapely skeleton of branches in winter (bottom right). It has earned its place in my garden where other trees have failed to impress.

Winter

As the flesh
withers on
the bones, the
garden's skeleton
now becomes
apparent; a gaunt
spectacle, but one
that is hopefully
not devoid of
its own spare
charms ...

Introduction

There are those who do not cross the threshold of their garden between the months of November and March, saving up their enthusiasm for spring when, once again, the bare soil shows evidence of life. For them, winter is a no-go zone and wellingtons are for those who live deep in the country among rutted tracks and by-ways made impassable by mud. But enough about Fulham …

For someone whose favourite season is spring, winter could be (and, to be honest, sometimes is) a time of deep depression. Day after day of leaden skies, low light levels and squelching journeys to open up and close down the chicken coop can take their toll. I yearn for a glimmer of light; I can almost, *almost*, understand why someone would pay to lie on a sunbed and have their skin bombarded by the coruscating rays of a dubious lamp.

But on bright days, when the skeletons of trees are silhouetted against a sky of forget-me-not blue, when the low angle of the sun makes you squint and shield your eyes, when the air is crisp and refreshes we outdoor types by the lungful, there is a lot to be said for a pause in the proceedings.

Much is made nowadays of the need for instant gratification. The sad fact is that it has the effect of removing one of life's greatest pleasures – that of anticipation. Winter is neatly crafted by the Almighty to redress that balance; to make Britons pause and take stock; rest even, and think about next year – hopefully rather than reluctantly.

If I grow a touch philosophical it is because winter offers me the time to do so. Spring and summer are seasons of rushing and catching up; there is little time to think; to consider. Oh, I know that in July and August I should be sitting on a bench in the garden and admiring the view; and I do, but only briefly. Something catches my eye – the fish need feeding, a weed needs pulling up, a deadhead removing – and I am off with my secateurs or my trowel and the second half of the cup of coffee goes cold in the Emma Bridgewater mug.

But in winter, the weeds grow more slowly or not at all, and I can gain ground while they sleep, hopefully finding myself ahead of the game come March. At least, that's the theory. Of course, I never am – not quite. There is always something that just gets away from me. But next year: ah, next year will be different; next year will be better.

As the leaves fall, autumn slips imperceptibly into winter; frost rimes the low box hedges and even faded border perennials can look attractive when dusted with ice crystals.

If the grey, damp days get me down, the cold and frosty ones perk me up, even if it does mean that I cannot walk across the lawn without my folly being highlighted a week later by the brown footprints that give away my track. But I can still admire the hoar frost on the branches of trees and the elegant riming on box and yew. Cobwebs take on a magic all their own, showing off the spinning skills of the hundred or more species of spider that inhabit the British garden.

Gales at this time of year do not give rise to the worry that they did in summer and autumn, when trees, like galleons in full sail on a stormy sea, were in danger of losing limbs or being blown over. Now they are neatly reefed in and put up less resistance. And the cold? It will help reduce the number of pests that survive the winter, won't it? Well, I have my doubts. Really severe winters might reduce the numbers of those pathogens that survive, but winters where temperatures fall below zero only occasionally are unlikely to make any real dent on the slug and snail population, especially if the molluscs have had the sense to hide themselves away in crevices in walls and in leafmould at the base of hedges. They are not stupid; they can feel the weather getting colder and make ample provision. But it suits us to think of winter iciness as a cauterisation of the garden and a cleanser of ills.

In many ways it is; it allows diseased foliage to be cleared away and disposed of, borders to be tidied, trees and shrubs to be pruned. And it also means that we gardeners can believe, albeit for just a few months, that we are, after all, in charge of our well-tamed patch of land. For now. 🌱

Garden objects take on a sculptural significance after snowfall, be they watering cans (left) or box and yew topiary (right).

The meadow

In spring I cannot wait for the meadow to grow; it seems to show a different face each year, and there is no doubt that the months of May, June and July show it off at its richest as the spring flowers give way to those of high summer. The make-up of this tapestry of flowers is ever changing, both with the seasons and with the years, and so it is never boring. But by September it has become a hayfield and after five months of glory any kind of definition has gone, and most of the species the meadow contains have shed their seeds. The hay is cut, the mower put over what remains, and the once knee-to-waist-high meadow spends the winter with a grade-one haircut.

Somehow the field seems smaller now. The hares that grazed the rides in summer and became ever bolder as the weeks went by are plainly visible when they dare to show themselves. Now there is no long grass in which they can hide and they must take to the hedgerow, which is garlanded with rose hips and haws, old man's beard and the black fruits of dogwood.

But I still enjoy my morning and evening walks, and the grass here is rough enough to cope with footprints in frosty weather. Overlying chalk, while making the ground squelch when wet, seldom becomes as slippery or as quagmire-like as clay. After a few days of dry weather it will become firm again and the walking easier.

Winter is a time of silhouettes – especially in late afternoon when the sun goes down, sometimes flooding the meadow in a pinkish glow.

The moment will come when I cut the hedge – leaving as many of the berries behind as I can and trying to time the operation so that the birds have not started prospecting for nests. It's always a difficult decision, but if the hedge were to grow higher than my head then the view of the field beyond would be blocked and our outlook not nearly so enjoyable. It's a juggling of priorities – ours and those of the wildlife – but then that's what gardening always is; a compromise, and hopefully a happy one.

Snowfall is delightfully indiscriminate and changes the face of everything in the garden, from sculptures and furniture to trees, shrubs and water features.

The south garden

It might be forecast, but sometimes, in spite of the fact that the weather affects my daily life to a considerable degree, I am unaware of the imminent arrival of snow. Waking up in the morning in our east-facing bedroom, two things give it away – the ringing silence and the brilliant intensity of the morning light. I love that moment of pulling up the window blind and seeing the whole garden below smothered in a pristine bright-white blanket. The camera is out, the garden toured, and then the job of knocking the snow from topiary specimens and evergreens begins.

I would love to leave them snow-capped and white-domed, but I know that, come the thaw, the light and powdery snow will turn as heavy as lead and branches will snap under the increased weight. I pull a shepherd's crook from the umbrella stand in the hall and make my foray into the winter wonderland, leaving as much of the snow underfoot unmarked as I can, while stroking it from box and yew, Portugal laurel and holly.

Most other plants will not turn a hair; a covering of snow insulates them from the kind of winter weather they really detest – prolonged sogginess which causes them to rot. Snow is dry until the thaw comes, and then its melting may well be rapid – a good watering that is preferable to months of muddy earth.

There are two other advantages of snow: the tattiest bits of the garden are transformed overnight – even building sites take on clean lines. And with snow covering bed and border, lawn and pond, there is simply nothing you can do. Have a rest. Curl up by the fire with a seed catalogue, or go to the potting shed to sharpen and oil your tools. Ah, yes; even when snow covers the ground there is *something* you can be getting on with. Killjoy …

The snow remains on the evergreens only until the photography is done, lest the thaw should break branches and ruin shapes.

The birds are
hungry now,
and my seed
bins empty with
increased rapidity.
Robins and
blackbirds wait
impatiently if
I take a lie in ...

The dolphin pond

The fountain goes off in winter – until a mild day when I am bored and want a bit of movement and activity about me. Then I turn it on for an hour or two, telling myself that the box below it will suffer if it remains saturated for too long. Sometimes I forget to turn it off, and the ice patterns are spectacular. But the spectacle now, if it qualifies as such, is from the evergreen box kerbs that delineate the shape of the garden and the topiary specimens that hover above it. In winter they take on their greatest role – that of giving the garden form, shape and interest when deciduous trees and shrubs are bare and border perennials have been cut to the ground. Without them my garden would be a dreary place between the months of November and March – almost half the year.

I've never regretted going rather overboard on topiary. Yes, it does mean that we always seem to be clipping something between June and September, but freshly clipped topiary is as satisfying to behold as a newly mown lawn and, if cleverly timed, needs doing only once a year as opposed to once a week. In winter especially, the shadow-play of the taller specimens means that the view changes by the hour and the garden really does seem to be mobile, rather than a static patch of ground which sees the sun rise and set with no significant change in appearance.

Some of the garden ornaments are taken under cover in winter, but others are tough enough to remain outdoors. Not possessing valuable Greek marbles *à la* Sissinghurst, I do not have to gaze on ugly canvas covers in winter. Mind you, I could probably fit one in somewhere …

And that is a real problem each winter – there is too much time to think about how I could spend more money on the garden.

The boy with dolphin (left) and two geese (right) – tough enough to withstand the winter weather outdoors, though sometimes I can hear their teeth chattering.

The west garden

I cannot deny that the garden to the west of the house is at its most interesting in summer. Most folk, after all, plan their garden with summer in mind. It's understandable (except when a summer like 2012 comes along, when it rains almost daily from April to late July and the barbecue season is somewhat curtailed).

If a garden does not look good in June it is never going to look good, usually because most folk go to their local nursery or garden centre in May and June and buy and plant what is in flower at that time. There is a simple solution: make a trip to the garden centre in every month of the year to buy something in flower or something eye-catching. This will ensure that a garden has at least a modicum of interest all the year round.

Evergreens are invaluable, provided they are not used in quantities that are redolent of the local cemetery. The box 'spats' around my avenue of pear trees never seem to me to look funereal, but some folk have a natural aversion to evergreens borne of a childhood fear of graveyards.

In winter it is understandably harder to find spectacular brilliance, bark and berries apart, but well-chosen garden ornaments can do their bit during the dreary months, sinking more into the background when spring and summer foliage diminishes their impact or partially shields them from open view.

I like garden ornaments – as focal points and as highlights – but they do need to be chosen with care. There is, I know, no accounting for taste, and it is entirely up to you what you use as decoration in your garden.

I'm no snob, but I can't pluck up much enthusiasm for overly vivid ceramic containers and brightly coloured gravel or glass paths. Wind chimes drive me nuts. I'd far rather listen to the sound of the wind in the willows or the chirruping of the birdies in the sycamore trees than endure the bings and bongs of some new-age confection crafted from copper pipe and baler twine.

Funnily enough, garden gnomes are not nearly so offensive as green-tinted damsels who look as though they've just been goosed in the shrubbery. And price is no guarantee of good taste – I've seen some astonishingly gruesome ornaments at the Chelsea Flower Show with a price tag well into five figures.

The garden gnomes? Well, there is a certain honesty to them which in the odd cottage garden (only the odd one) can have a certain charm. They are, however, unlikely to be championed by the garden designers at the Chelsea Flower Show.

Garden ornaments and the seedheads of perennials provide particular interest in winter when the garden is denuded of leaf and colour. Snow adds its own magic.

The greenhouse in winter

There are times when I dream of having a proper 'winter garden', under cover, where I could plant a chair and read among the orchids and the ferns, the Indian azaleas and orange blossom. But then commonsense bites and I think of the size of the heating bill. As a result, in winter my greenhouse plays host to plants which need no more than frost protection to come through unscathed – favourite scented-leafed pelargoniums, a massive tender fern that goes outdoors in summer, some spectacular aeoniums and a huge white-flowered jasmine which has taken root in one corner. There are humeas – the incense plants – their leaves brown and drying now, their fuse-wire-thin trails of minute crimson flowers desiccated but still giving off a hint of their summer fragrance of high-church worship. They are not spectacular plants to look at, but they give my greenhouse its own unique perfume. I collect the seeds for next year's batch and sigh at their passing.

I do have a propagating frame where more heat can be given economically, thanks to the provision of electricity, a tight lid and a thermostat, but seed-sowing does not begin in earnest until February, so in winter I take care to pick off faded leaves and flowers from the long-term residents to prevent fungal diseases from spreading, and I avoid overwatering at all costs. It all sounds a bit deadly. But I do make plans at this time, for the new things I will try, while the old, fat begonia corms are drying on their sides in their pots of dry compost under the bench.

Soon I will struggle to accommodate all the things I want to grow next year, and I'll remember, as I do annually, that however large my greenhouse it will always be filled to overflowing.

The greenhouse itself is a valued piece of garden architecture at this time. Made by Alitex from powder-coated aluminium, it has the benefit of being relatively maintenance-free (washing down and the oiling of hinges is the only regular care it needs) but it also looks handsome and in keeping with a 300-year-old house – the elegance of an older structure with none of the high maintenance associated with timber, putty and paint.

It sits at the end of its path directly in line with the kitchen window and reminds me, all through the winter, that it is the proportions and the lines in my garden that give me the greatest pleasure. Angles and vistas and axes and focal points are never more in evidence than in the quiet months.

This may be the least eventful of the four seasons in my garden, but it is not without its satisfaction. The pleasures are quieter, but deeply felt for all that. 🌱

The greenhouse in winter, snug under a blanket of snow, its inhabitants ticking over and hopefully surviving ...

The south terrace through the seasons

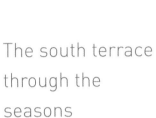

The changes happen imperceptibly, but the fact that the garden adjusts its livery through the year points up the differing pleasures of the seasons. In winter (main picture) it is tempting to leave snow in its pristine state, but it must be brushed from evergreens before it thaws, increases in weight dramatically and snaps off their branches. In spring (top right) life returns with fresh green shoots and the disappearance of dull grey soil. Summer (centre right) is a time of abundant growth and judicious trimming to avoid the welter of foliage overwhelming the garden's shape and form. And autumn (bottom right) is 'dustpan and brush' time – the clearing up after the final burst of colour.

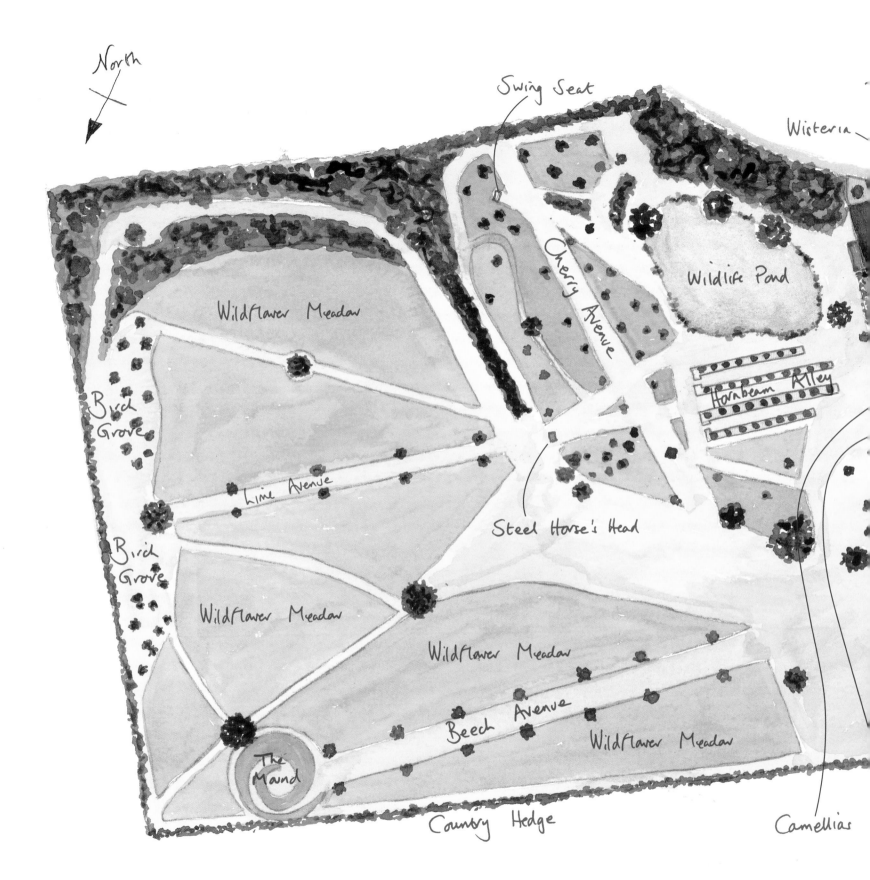

North

Swing Seat

Wisteria

Wildlife Pond

Cherry Avenue

Wildflower Meadow

Hornbeam Alley

Birch Grove

Lime Avenue

Birch Grove

Steel Horse's Head

Wildflower Meadow

Wildflower Meadow

Beech Avenue

Wildflower Meadow

The Mound

Country Hedge

Camellias

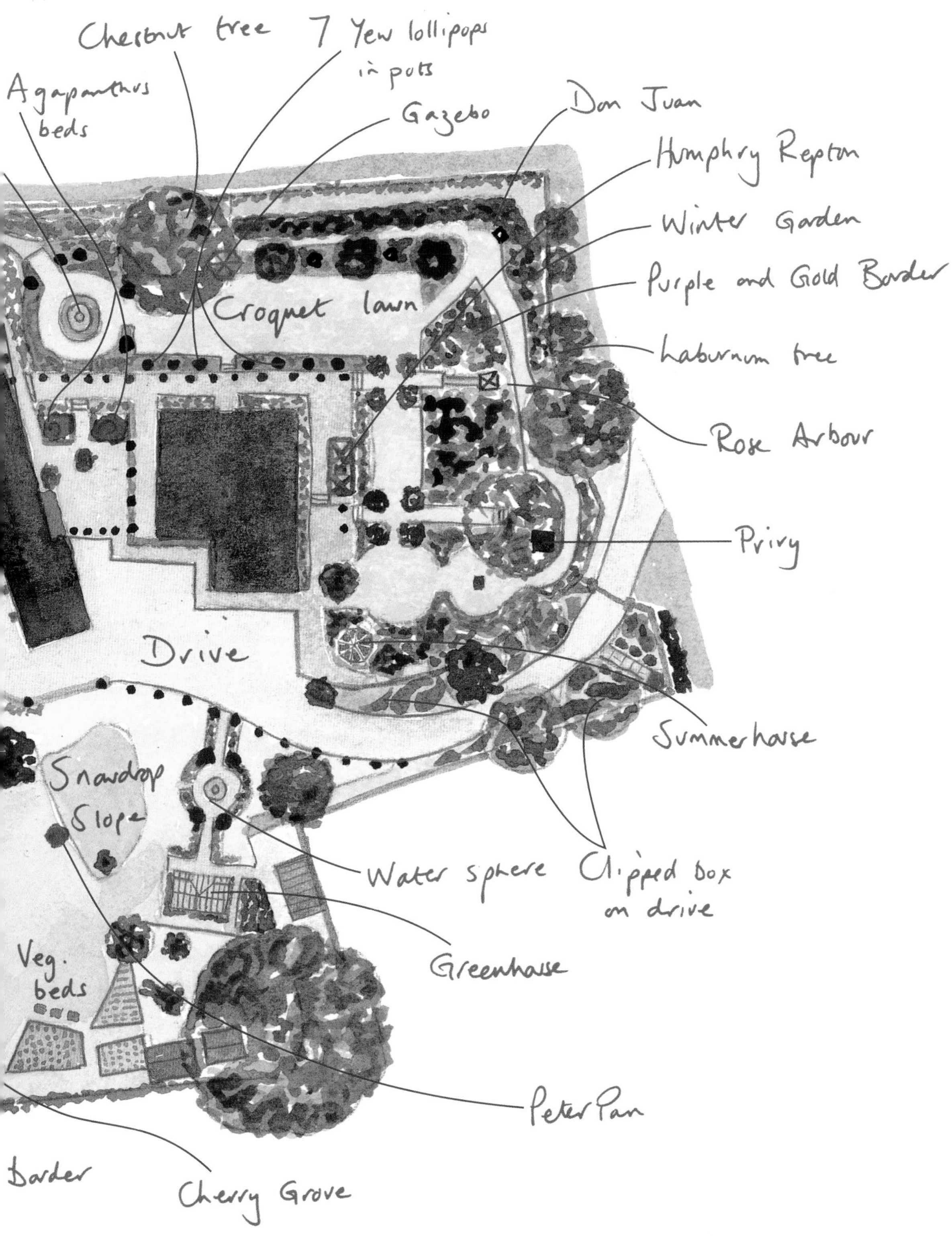

My Secret Garden

This is how the garden and the wildflower meadow look ten years after we moved in. The bones are established now, but the unpicking and replanting go on – that's the interesting bit …

———

Chestnut tree

7 Yew lollipops in pots

Agapanthus beds

Gazebo

Don Juan

Humphry Repton

Winter Garden

Purple and Gold Border

Laburnum tree

Croquet lawn

Rose Arbour

Privy

Drive

Summerhouse

Snowdrop Slope

Water sphere

Clipped box on drive

Veg. beds

Greenhouse

Peter Pan

Border

Cherry Grove

Plan of the garden drawn by the author

Index

Acknowledgements

Gardening can be a solitary pursuit, and is none the worse for that. I enjoy quietly working among my beds and borders, standing behind a lawn mower, pruning or deadheading, alone with my thoughts. But without the help of all sorts of people my garden – and my gardening – would be considerably less rewarding and, I have to admit, less successful.

Sue Richards and Bill Budd have worked with me now for around thirty years – we have all three lost count of the precise duration. They laboured on through the *Gardeners' World* years, readying beds, borders and assorted equipment for filming. They continue to anticipate, alleviate and encourage in equal measure and without them I could not manage to live the life I do. They make the going easier and my debt to them and my long-suffering PA Caroline Mitchell (who manages my impossible diary) is immeasurable.

My family, too, have been enduringly patient and supportive when prevented from enjoying their domestic freedom by cameras and film crews, as well as tolerating my moments of despair when box blight strikes or pigeons wreak havoc. I can only hope that the garden that has resulted is some kind of compensation.

There are others whose input has been of tremendous value. Trevor Bell, our architect, could be forgiven for being exasperated which, from time to time, I know he is. He never shows it and continues to solve tricky structural and design problems in unrealistic time frames.

Taff Garland, Elliott Warner, Phil Burmingham and Jamie Stickler have all helped with building work, and Gavin Edmunds is a matchless tree surgeon who keeps anything above what I consider a comfortable height in good order while displaying the acrobatic prowess of an orang-utan. He is also considerably better looking.

Robert Smith is a talented blacksmith whose efficiency is matched by his skill and his calm approach – all our ironmongery and our garden stakes have been crafted in his smithy – and

Jamie Brand unfailingly manages to turn my woodworking imaginings into reality. Colin Kinch transformed an unpromising pile of earth into a carefully sculpted mound from which we can now survey our 'estate'.

Laurence Budd comes and quietly cracks on with the mowing when the rest of us are up to our ears in other things, and Alex Budd, too, is on call as an extra pair of hands when the going gets tough. Our neighbouring farmer Sean Baddeley has provided much help over the years, and Dave Redman can be relied on to appear on cue with a tractor and trailer when our own transport falls short of the required muscle and horsepower.

My thanks go to Kate Bradbury, who was kind enough to come and monitor my bumblebee population and generous enough to provide a brief synopsis for this book. Laura Richards is expert in the care of wildlife of another kind – she looks after our hens – and Spud the cat – whenever we cannot.

To Jim Keeling, Nic Fiddian Green, Martin Cook, Fergus Wessel, Ian Gill, Claire Tupman, Paul Amey and Dick Budden I owe a debt of gratitude for their artistic and sculptural endeavours, which enrich my life on a daily basis, and to the nurseries and garden centres, seedsmen and growers...well, this is turning into an Oscar acceptance speech, but I really am grateful to them all.

Lorna Russell encouraged and cajoled me into writing this book, and Joe Cottington has been of tremendous editorial help. But my main thanks go to Jonathan Buckley without whose photographs this book would hardly have been worth writing. He is a matchless snapper and a great chum.

The faults, the lapses of horticultural taste, the moments of boastfulness and any shortcomings are my own. But I love my garden, and hope that some of my passion might rub off. To paraphrase Salman Rushdie: 'If you don't like my garden, you can always go and make your own.' I hope that you do – on both counts.

10 9 8 7 6 5 4 3 2 1

Published in 2012 by BBC Books, an imprint of Ebury Publishing
A Random House Group company

All text by Alan Titchmarsh

Text © Alan Titchmarsh 2012
Photographs © Jonathan Buckley 2012

Alan Titchmarsh has asserted his right to be identified as the author of this Work in accordance with the Copyright, Designs and Patents Act 1988.

All rights reserved. No part of this publication may be reproduced, stored in a retrieval system, or transmitted in any form or by any means, electronic, mechanical, photocopying, recording or otherwise, without the prior permission of the copyright owner.

The Random House Group Limited Reg. No. 954009

Addresses for companies within the Random House Group can be found at www.randomhouse.co.uk

A CIP catalogue record for this book is available from the British Library

ISBN 978 1 849 90058 4

MIX
Paper from responsible sources
FSC® C015829
FSC www.fsc.org

The Random House Group Limited supports The Forest Stewardship Council (FSC®), the leading international forest certification organisation. Our books carrying the FSC label are printed on FSC® certified paper. FSC is the only forest certification scheme endorsed by the leading environmental organisations, including Greenpeace. Our paper procurement policy can be found at www.randomhouse.co.uk/environment

Commissioning editor: Lorna Russell
Project editor: Joe Cottington
Copy editor: Helena Caldon
Designer: Andrew Barron/thextension
Production: Phil Spencer

Printed and bound in Italy by Printer Trento S.r.l.
Colour origination by XY Digital Ltd

To buy books by your favourite authors and register for offers, visit www.randomhouse.co.uk